Lost
Knowledge
of the
Imagination

Lost Knowledge
of the
Imagination

GARY LACHMAN

Floris Books

For Kathleen Raine (1908-2003), who showed the way

First published by Floris Books in 2017
Second printing 2018

© 2017 Gary Lachman

Gary Lachman has asserted his right under the
Copyright, Design and Patents Act 1988
to be identified as the Author of this Work

MIX
Paper from
responsible sources
FSC   FSC® C013056
www.fsc.org

 Also available as an eBook

British Library CIP Data available
ISBN 978-178250-445-0
Printed in Great Britain
by TJ International

Contents

Acknowledgments

My thanks go to my editor Christopher Moore for taking on the project and to the staff of the British Library where most of the research was done. I'd like to thank the students who took my class in 'The Lost Knowledge of the Imagination', given for the Californian Institute of Integral Studies, for help in working through some of the ideas, and I'd also like to thank Alfonso Montouri who suggested I give the course as part of CIIS' Transformative Studies programme. My sons Joshua and Max and their mother Ruth helped in their usual way. But my very special thanks goes to my collaborator Anja Bjorlo, who suggested the idea and contributed the index.

London, August 2017

Chapter One
A Different Kind of Knowing

In the early seventeenth century, a new way of knowing and understanding ourselves and the world we live in appeared in the West and quickly rose to prominence. So effective and powerful was this new approach to knowledge that within a relatively short time – merely a few centuries – it achieved ascendancy in practically all fields of human endeavour, and subsequently became, as it is today, the gauge by which we measure such difficult and fundamental notions as 'truth' and 'reality'. A few centuries may not seem like a short time, but if we compare the changes that have taken place in human existence since this new way of knowing first raised its head, to the millennia that preceded it, we will not be exaggerating too greatly if we feel that something like a 'revolution' had occurred. As more than one historian has pointed out, human life, even that of the planet itself, has changed more in the four centuries since the arrival of this new mode of knowing, than in the long ages that came before it. What happened in the first years of the seventeenth century was no gradual development, no addition to what had gone before, but a complete break with the past and a radical new beginning.

To be sure, the roots of this new way of knowing could be traced back to earlier times. Its origins can be seen in Greek philosophy, in Plato and Aristotle. But they go back even further, and can be found in much earlier thinkers, such as Thales, Anaximander, Pythagoras, and the other pre-Socratic philosophers who appeared around the eastern Mediterranean in the centuries around 500 BC. This was the period that the German existential philosopher Karl Jaspers christened the 'Axial Age'. Jaspers assigned a unique importance to this age because he argued that it was during it that 'the spiritual foundations of humanity were laid', a development that took place across the globe.[1] During Jaspers' Axial Age, Confucius and Lao-Tse appeared in China; India saw the creation of the Upanishads and the appearance of the Buddha; Zoroaster emerged in Persia and laid the groundwork of Zoroastrianism, which saw the world as a battleground between the cosmic forces of good and evil; and in the Holy Lands, the Hebrew prophets arose, preaching a new relationship between God and his creation.

It was during this time that in Greece a new kind of individual, moved by new interests and sensibilities, appeared. While in other parts of the globe the Axial Age saw the appearance of powerful religious and ethical feelings and insights that would inform whole civilisations, in Greece and Asia Minor – that part of modern Turkey bordering the Mediterranean Sea – something different occurred. Here what we can call a movement from a 'mythical' to a 'mental' outlook took place. A new kind of character, the 'thinker', appeared for the first time, what the philosopher Edmund Husserl called 'theoretical man'. This new type of character had a strange *impersonal* curiosity about the world around him. As the literary critic George Steiner put it, unlike most people around him, he found himself 'interested in something for its own enigmatic sake', and not for the practical reasons that until then had motivated most human inquiry.[2] That this is still the case today is not too difficult to confirm.

For such a person, the old myths concerning the creation of the world that they found in Homer and Hesiod were no longer satisfying. They were not interested in a narrative explaining how the world came to be, or the supernatural origin of other elements in this world. What Thales of Miletus or his student Anaximander and other thinkers much like them wanted to know was what the world was *made of*. According to the philosopher John Shand, they were looking for 'the original and controlling stuff and first principle of the universe, the nature of which provides an explanation of the existing universe, and its origin, as a whole'.[3] For Thales this was water. For Anaximenes, a younger contemporary of Anaximander, it was air. Later sages had other ideas. Heraclitus – called the 'dark philosopher' because of his gnomic sayings – believed the 'original and controlling stuff' was fire. Other thinkers had similar suggestions.

We may not be impressed with these answers to what may seem to us childish attempts to 'explain' the universe, even if Thales, Anaximenes and the others had substantial arguments to support their theories. But the impetus behind them carries on today. We see this when the world's media becomes very excited at the discovery of yet another sub-atomic particle even more elementary than the last, that will supposedly allow us to finally solve the 'mystery' of existence – until, that is, the next particle turns up.

Closer to the seventeenth century, we can say the new mode of knowing that I am speaking of arose out of the renewed interest in Nature as an object of study and contemplation, that presaged the rise of the Gothic in the twelfth century. Round about AD 862, John Scotus Eriugena, an Irish monk and theologian, wrote a work called *De divisione Naturae (On the Divisions of Nature)*. Eriugena – the name means 'born in Ireland' – had earlier translated from Greek into Latin a work by an anonymous Syrian monk who most likely lived circa AD 500.[4] *The Celestial Hierarchy* combined the Neoplatonic philosophy that had flourished centuries earlier in Alexandria in Egypt with the nascent theology of early Christianity to create the great panoply of spiritual beings – Seraphim and Cherubim down to the angels – that inhabit the Christian universe. Eriugena absorbed this Neoplatonic influence and through it he began to see Nature in a different light, something that comes through in his work. Rather than relegate the natural world to the unredeemed pagans or, worse, the devil, as had been the case for centuries, he recognised within it the presence of the divine. He spoke of nature's 'manifest theophanies' – God's appearance within it.

To the later scholars of the School of Chartres in the twelfth century, these appearances were most recognisable in what became known as 'sacred geometry'. This was exemplified in formulae like the 'golden section', or *phi,* that they found embodied in different forms throughout nature, and which was used in constructing many Gothic cathedrals. From the *Timaeus* – one of the few works of Plato available to them – they learned that God was a geometer and mathematician. As it had been for Plato – and even more for his predecessor Pythagoras – number became a way of grasping the divine. Images of the Creator using a compass appeared on cathedrals, with Pythagoras himself finding a place on the west portal of one of the most magnificent examples of sacred geometry to appear in any age, the cathedral at Chartres.

It must be clear by now to the reader that the 'new way of knowing' I have been writing about was what we have come to know as science. Like the first sages of ancient Greece, around the first years of the seventeenth century, individuals began to appear who were curious about the world in a way that was strikingly and disturbingly different. Like their Greek predecessors, they wanted to know what made the world tick – an anachronistic phrase here that would soon prove worryingly apt. Two centuries earlier the Renaissance filled many bold spirits with the belief that man was something more than the lowly, sinful creature of the Middle Ages, forever in danger of wandering off the path of redemption and finding his way to the temptations of Satan. The rediscovery of the works of sages like Plato and even more those of the supposed founder of all learning, the celebrated Hermes Trismegistus, gave the creative spirits of the Renaissance a renewed sense of human potential. Man was able to choose his own path; he was no longer held back by the limitations and constraints of dogma and fear. He was a creative force. There was a sense that man, in his own way, was really something of a god. He was certainly more vitally endowed and strategically placed than the angels, a belief given vivid expression in a representative work of the time, Pico della Mirandola's *Oration on the Dignity of Man*.

This stirring confidence and incentive now informed a new breed of genius. Like the mages of the Renaissance, they believed in humankind's ability to understand their world, to free themselves from the shackles of ignorance and fear. And like the scholars of Chartres, they believed that number was essential to this endeavour. Number, as Pythagoras had said long ago, was indeed behind everything. It was. But for these new men, it wasn't in the way that Pythagoras had believed.

For Pythagoras, numbers had a metaphysical reality; they were symbols or expressions of certain *qualities*, certain fundamental characteristics or essences that provided the pattern and shape of reality. There was a quality of what we would call 'twoness' just as there was a quality of 'threeness'. Pythagoras and his followers summed up this insight in a figure they called the *tetraktys*, which encompassed the entire universe in a pyramid formed of ten dots. In this way they showed how through certain stages, the physical world emerges from the undifferentiated One. A later variant of this belief can be found in the Kabbalah, the esoteric tradition of Judaism, as well as in Neoplatonism.

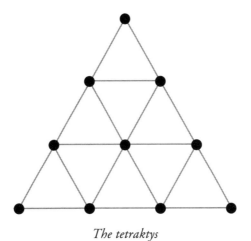

The tetraktys

Number was understood in what we might call this mystical way for some time, but with the rise of the new way of knowing, this changed. From housing qualities and archetypes of reality, number came to be seen as primarily an agent of measurement. Through a strange, brief, but effective collaboration, the Church and a rising science, soon to be sworn enemies, temporarily worked together to empty the world of its qualitative character, of what the philosopher of language Owen Barfield calls its 'insides'.[5] What remained was its 'outside', its physical form, its surface, which, it was increasingly understood, was subject to what were beginning to be called 'the laws of nature'. These laws were of a purely physical character, the push and pull of mechanical cause and effect. At this point the idea of finding out what made the world 'tick' became something more than a metaphor. Increasingly it was seen that Creation was only the most grand form of a variety of mechanical devices – machines – that had recently captured western imagination. From a world of qualities what was emerging was one of quantity. And so vigorous was the pursuit of this new approach to number that what quickly came into effect was what the Traditionalist philosopher René Guénon called the 'Reign of Quantity'.

Such was the seismic shift in Western man's relationship to the world – the change came about later in other parts of the planet but has by now encircled the globe – that Jaspers argues that it was as 'incisive' an event in human history as his 'Axial Age'.[6] It is arguable that its effect has been even more profound, at least on the level of our material lives. It takes a small effort of imagination to recognise that the way in which the average person in the west lives today would have been inconceivable to anyone living prior to the 'scientific revolution'. We enjoy at easy grasp a technology that kings of an earlier time could not dream of, let alone possess. From smartphones to anaesthetics, automobiles to interstellar space probes, the 'reign of quantity' has produced remarkable results. No one denies this and only a fool or a confirmed luddite would believe we could in any positive sense return to a pre-technological world. I say 'positive sense' because we have no dearth of dystopian visions, apocalyptic anticipations of a soon-to-be-future in which our technological world comes crashing down around us, and we find ourselves, and not only metaphorically, back in the caves. It seems that for many, the only way to conceive of the world without technology is to end it.

And yet, it seems almost a cliché by now to point out that the power and mastery over the natural world that has come to us through the reign of quantity, and which we turn more and more on ourselves, has come at a very high price. The emptying of the 'inside' of the world – and increasingly ourselves – that was necessary in order for the new way of knowing to take root, has not been an unalloyed success. While at first a necessary stage in humankind's development – or so I see it – the power over the natural world that has come into our hands has in recent times begun to show its shadow side. Global warming, urbanisation, industrialisation and the environmental and social problems that arise with them, as well as a variety of other crises facing us today, have their roots in the kind of mastery over the physical world that arrived with our new way of knowing. But as pressing and urgent as these challenges are – and I have mentioned only a few of them merely as an indication of their nature – they are not the only unforeseen side effects of the 'knowledge revolution' four centuries ago.

Our own 'inside' has been dramatically affected by it too. The freedom of mind that was achieved by jettisoning dogma and faith had a dual effect. It liberated the human mind, but it also seemed to set it adrift. One of the results of the new way of knowing is that it has left many of us feeling, as the novelist Walker Percy put it, 'lost in the cosmos'. Man, in his ignorance, had believed he was the centre of the universe. Our new knowledge disabused us of this misconception. We are not at the centre. We occupy a modest position near a mid-range star in one arm of one galaxy, itself full of billions of other stars, set in a universe full of billions of other galaxies. And for all we know, there are billions of other universes.

We began to lose our moorings in the mid-sixteenth century when Copernicus set the sun loose from the earth and we began, as the philosopher Nietzsche said, 'rolling from the centre toward X'.[7] The success the new way of knowing had in disabusing us of any idea that we are in any way necessary, important, or essential to the universe is perhaps best expressed in a remark by the respected astrophysicist Steven Weinberg. In *The First Three Minutes*, his book about what happened immediately after the Big Bang, Weinberg writes, 'The more the universe seems comprehensible, the more it also seems pointless'.[8] Comprehensible here means quantifiable. It does not take much to infer from this that we, the inhabitants of this pointless but quantified universe are, unavoidably, even more pointless.

Anomie, apathy, alienation, a sense of existential 'So what?' accompanied the success of our now seemingly unstoppable aim of quantifying all of existence and our experience of it. The quantification of human existence was carried out in different ways, with disciplines once considered part of the 'humanities' now adopting the effective methods of the new way of knowing. The itch to obtain the same kind of 'objective' 'measurable' results that the 'hard' sciences were achieving made their 'softer' relations jealous, and so increasingly practically all forms of scholarship, research, inquiry, and study aped the new approach. What this meant was that science was quickly becoming, or giving birth to, 'Scientism'. This, according to the eminent historian Jacques Barzun, is 'the fallacy of believing that the method of science must be used on all forms of experience and, given time, will settle every issue'.[9]

Although since the rise of the new way of knowing many have taken argument with its misuse and obvious inadequacies in dealing with many forms of experience – we will meet some of these critics as we go along – for the most part 'Scientism' is the dominant 'belief system' – less abstractly, religion – of modern times. When we want answers to the 'mysteries' of the universe, or of ourselves, we don't go to philosophers, poets, mystics, or priests. We go to scientists, many of whom, it seems to me, are only too happy to provide confident, convincing answers even if they have as much idea about the mystery as anyone else.

Barzun points out that at its beginning someone well trained in the new way of knowing, and who was blessed with a natural talent for it, was also prescient enough to recognise that if not used wisely it could lead to problems. Blaise Pascal was born in 1623 and it was not long before he was recognised as a prodigy; at the age of twelve he was sitting in on mathematics discussions with the philosopher René Descartes, regarded as one of the founders of the modern world, and a brilliant exponent of the new way of knowing. Pascal was a mathematician, logician, physicist, and inventor; experiments he conducted led to the invention of the barometer, and he devised the first calculating machine, known as *La Pascaline*, something he whipped up to help his father, a tax collector. But Pascal was also a religious philosopher and what we can call an early existentialist. And although he was not a mystic, as he is often described, he did have at least one mystical experience, the import of which he had written down and had sewn into his coat; it was only upon his death that it was discovered. It was headed by one word, 'fire', and spoke of 'tears of joy'. Its gist was that he believed in the 'living God' of Abraham, Isaac, and Jacob, not the bloodless abstraction of the 'scholars and philosophers'.[10]

Also after his death a collection of notes Pascal had made for a book defending Christianity against the rising 'freethinkers' – exponents of the new way of knowing – were discovered. These have come down to us as his *Pensées*, 'Thoughts'. Famously in them he voiced what to our ears strikes the familiar note of cosmic anxiety. Looking at the vast strange universe revealed through the 'scientific method', Pascal remarked that 'the eternal silence of these infinite spaces terrifies me'. It seems that well before Steven Weinberg, Pascal was concerned about our comprehensible, but pointless, existence.

But in his *Pensées* Pascal also voiced a concern about the new way of knowing that had opened the curtains on the spaces that terrified him.

At the beginning of the *Pensées* Pascal writes about the differences between what he calls the 'mathematical and intuitive mind', or the *esprit géométrique* and the *esprit de finesse*, the 'spirit of geometry' and the 'spirit of finesse'.[11] As Barzun explains, the spirit of geometry 'works with exact definitions and abstractions in science or mathematics', while the spirit of finesse 'works with ideas and perceptions not capable of exact definition'.[12] There is no debate over the definition of a right-angle triangle or gravity, Barzun points out, while things like love, freedom, poetry and other meaningful but less exact phenomena are not so well defined. The spirit of geometry works sequentially, reasoning its way step-by-step, following its rules, whereas the intuitive minds sees everything all at once. It arrives at its goal in one glance, not by a process of deduction.

The drawback here is that because the lack of definition is rooted in its subjects themselves, and not due to insufficient information or 'facts' about them – when will we have all the facts about love or freedom? – those who follow the spirit of finesse find it difficult, if not impossible, to explain *how* they know what they know. There are no steps 1, 2, and 3; it just hits them and it is obvious, self-evident. We hear a sonata by Beethoven and we *know* it is beautiful and meaningful; we do not arrive at this knowledge through a series of logical steps. We do not say to ourselves, 'Well, it has *x* number of notes in this passage, which means that ...' and so on. But if asked how we know it is beautiful and meaningful, and even worse, if we can prove it, we draw a blank. The spirit of geometry can take us by the hand and lead us from definition, theorem, and axiom to the goal. But the process is mechanical, practically tautological, as each definition is merely another way of stating the same thing (4 is only another way of saying 2 + 2). And it works best with practical, utilitarian things, not with those that have a purchase on our emotional being.

Pascal was admirably equipped to follow mathematical reasoning, but he knew of other reasoning too; as he famously wrote, 'the heart has its reasons that reason does not know'. It knows them through the spirit of *finesse,* the intuitive approach, one of the two directions, as Barzun says, that the 'one human mind can take'.[13]

Pascal's distinction between the spirit of geometry and the spirit of finesse has been voiced in different ways at different times by different thinkers. A few centuries before Pascal, St Thomas Aquinas posed his own distinction between 'kinds of knowledge'. He called the 'lower' knowledge that was achieved through reasoning the 'active search' for knowledge, while the 'higher' kind, intellect, was 'the intuitive possession of it'.[14] Some centuries after Pascal, in his unclassifiable work *The Adventurous Heart,* the German writer Ernst Jünger spoke of something he called 'the master key'. 'Our understanding is such,' Jünger writes, 'that it is able to engage from the circumference as well as at the midpoint. For the first case, we possess ant-like industriousness, for the second, the gift of intuition.' Jünger goes on: 'For the mind that comprehends the midpoint, knowledge of the circumference becomes secondary – just as individual room keys lose importance for someone with the master key of a house.'[15]

Similarly, the philosopher Michael Polanyi differentiated between what he called 'tacit' and 'explicit' knowing. Explicit knowing is the kind we can relate step-by-step, as in a scientific experiment or a mathematical equation. Tacit knowing is implicit. It cannot be stated clearly in the same way as explicit knowing. It is the kind of knowing of which, as Polanyi says, 'we can know more than we can tell'.[16] You can spell out, step-by-step, the process of solving a quadratic equation; that is explicit knowledge, and we are subject to it throughout our school years. But if you try to explain to someone how to ride a bicycle, you will find it very difficult. You can show them how to do it; that's easy because it is tacit knowledge, knowledge you have but can't say much about. But you cannot explicitly say step-by-step what you do when you are showing them how to ride the bike. Most likely if you try to do this you will fall off. And that is how we learn to ride a bicycle in the first place. We don't 'half' ride it, then ride it a bit more, until we finally can ride it 'all the way'.[17] We find one day that suddenly we can, all at once. Some part of us other than our conscious mind has absorbed what we have learned and does it for us, what Colin Wilson calls 'the robot'. In fact, this absorption is 'learning'. And the knowledge remains, implicitly, unless we make the mistake of thinking about it too much. If I start to think about how I type I will soon lose track of what I want to type.

The philosopher Alfred North Whitehead recognised this when he said that: 'Civilisation advances by extending the number of important operations which we can perform without thinking about them'. Whitehead also made a distinction between two kinds of perception that share similarities with Polanyi's 'tacit' and 'explicit' knowing and Pascal's spirits of geometry and finesse. In *Symbolism: Its Meaning and Effect,* Whitehead speaks of 'immediacy perception' and 'meaning perception'.[18] Simply put, immediacy perception gives us the individual, immediate 'facts' of what we see, bit by bit, while meaning perception gives us the whole picture, all at once.

It is not too difficult to see that Whitehead's immediacy is well suited for the kind of quantitative knowing that came to prominence in the seventeenth century, and that 'meaning perception' is another way of talking about Ernst Jünger's 'master key'. Elsewhere I have written about Whitehead's work in the context of new developments in 'split-brain' psychology.[19] In *The Master and His Emissary* the literary scholar and neuroscientist Iain McGilchrist reboots the whole 'left brain/right brain' discussion, which had petered out in the 1990s when 'hard' neuroscientists were averse to being associated with something that had been taken up by pop psychology and New Age enthusiasts.

Another factor also turned serious research away from our split-brain. The neat separation and localisation of different psychological functions that had initially seemed the case when investigation into why we have two brains first began, fairly soon began to break down. When it appeared that, with most functions, both sides of our brain are involved – with emphasis in some things on one side or the other – scientists began to doubt whether there was any significant reason why we had two brains in the first place. Some even joked that one was a 'spare'. Yet what McGilchrist discovered is that while both sides of our brain may do the same things, they do them very differently. It was not a matter of *what* they did, he saw, but *how* they did it.

Put briefly, our right brain, which McGilchrist contends is older and primary – it is the 'master' of his title – sees the world as a whole, as a given totality, a living presence, much as we see another person. In Pascal's terms, it sees things intuitively, 'at a glance'. It is interested in implicit meanings. Because of this, its picture is somewhat vague, somewhat 'fuzzy'. It has a general, indubitable sense of 'meaning', yet it cannot articulate it in any detail – much like the implicit meanings in music that we cannot articulate explicitly. That is the job of the left brain, McGilchrist's 'emissary'.

It's business is to 'unpack' what the right brain 'presences', to 'spell it out', as it were, to focus on the individual trees that make up the forest given to it by the right brain – and eventually to focus on the individual leaves of a given tree. In Whitehead's terms, the right brain sees with 'meaning perception', while the left is concerned with 'immediacy perception'. We could also say that the left brain knows through Aquinas' 'active search' for knowledge, while the right has the 'intuitive possession' of it.

McGilchrist argues that throughout human history, the two 'ways' of our two brains complemented each other and worked, as democracies should, through a system of checks and balances, with each one inhibiting or compensating for the other's excesses in a kind of friendly rivalry. There have been times when one has gained a dominance, but these have always been evened out. And there have been times when both brains worked together creatively, in what I call a 'Goldilocks moment', when things are 'just right'. There is good reason to suspect that for millennia, something like a right brain dominance was the case, and that the shift in human consciousness that produced 'theoretical man' during Jaspers' 'Axial Age', was a movement toward giving the left brain more say.

What has happened though, McGilchrist argues, is that over the last two centuries – more specifically since the Industrial Revolution – the left brain has gained an increasing ascendancy over the right. Its determination to analyse experience, to break everything down into easily manageable bits and pieces, a necessary process for our survival, has got out of hand and is squeezing the right brain's contribution out of the picture. What has happened is that, as McGilchrist presents it, the 'emissary' has usurped power from the 'master', and has set itself up as the boss. What this has resulted in, McGilchrist argues, is an increasingly fragmented picture of the world, with less and less awareness of the intuitive glue, needed to hold things together.

The Industrial Revolution is the child, of course, of the 'knowledge revolution' of the early seventeenth century, with the reign of quantity giving birth to the kinds of technology that dominate us today. We can say that McGilchrist's left brain – not his own personal one, of course, although it, too, like our own, shares in this – has taken the new way of knowing and run with it.

But this puts the cart before the horse. The new way of knowing is rooted in the left brain, it is a product of it and it is, as we've seen, something that has been with us at least since the Axial Age. What has happened is that in the 'knowledge revolution' of the seventeenth century, through various factors, the new way of knowing – a heightened, intensified, and ruthless application of the curiosity of 'theoretical man' – made a successful bid to oust any competitors. The drive to quantify experience and to apply the results of this to practical ends began. The result of this is the modern world we see around us, and which McGilchrist believes is evidence of the left brain's bid to recreate the world 'in its own image', with any input from the right being marginalised, if not dismissed outright.

If McGilchrist is right, then we are truly suffering from a kind of schizophrenia, with one part of ourselves trying to excise the other – an 'other' which is as deeply rooted in us, if not more, as itself. As can immediately be seen, if this attempt is successful, it will result in a kind of suicide. At the very least we will suffer the kinds of self-antagonism that befell people who were subject to operations disconnecting one brain from the other, and who subsequently found themselves at war with their 'other half'.[20] In *Faust*, his classic tale of how the dominance of one kind of knowing can empty a life of all meaning and satisfaction, the great German Romantic poet Goethe said: 'Two souls, alas, live in my breast'. He may have got his anatomy wrong, but the insight is clear. Yet Goethe might have added: 'And they don't get along'.

If our brains are really battling it out – or, more accurately, if our right brain is being subjected to aggression from the left – then we are, I am afraid, in for some trouble. If our left brain, fired with a passion for the new way of knowing, succeeds in evicting its neighbour, then the result will be some new kind of being, that will be radically different from ourselves, or at least from how we are supposed to be. We would not have two brains if we did not need them and we would not need them if they did not work differently, with both approaches necessary for us to be 'fully human'.

McGilchrist was not the first to recognise this. More than a century ago the classicist Francis Cornford wrote a remarkable book, *From Religion to Philosophy*, that charted the shift from the 'mythic' to the 'mental' sensibility mentioned earlier. While Cornford recognised, as Jaspers did, that something monumental had taken place around the eastern side of the Mediterranean circa 500 BC, he also saw that our 'mythic consciousness' was not as thoroughly eliminated at that time as early historians of ideas believed. 'The philosophical Muse is not a motherless Athena,' Cornford wrote, referring to the myth of the birth of Athena, fully formed, from Zeus' brow, after it had been split open by Prometheus' axe. What this meant is that the new 'theoretical' approach grew out of mythic soil; it did not appear suddenly and was not unprecedented. Cornford argued that the new kind of consciousness that informed 'theoretical man' emerged from Greek religion and mythology. It did not jettison these last entirely, as forms of superstition and ignorance, as Cornford's contemporaries, and practically everyone else, believed it had, and were happy to do themselves.[21]

The new way of wondering about the world would eventually, as we've seen, become what we know as science. But it grew up in the company of another tradition. The two schools, Cornford saw, were 'moved by distinguishable impulses along lines diverging, more and more widely, towards opposite conclusions'. Writing in 1912, Cornford argued that these impulses 'are still operative in our own speculation, for the simple reason that they correspond to two permanent needs of human nature, and characterise two familiar types of human temperament'.[22] We seem to be back at Pascal's two spirits, and if there is any doubt, Cornford goes on to dot the i's and cross the t's. Speaking of the prevalence of the one tradition in his – and our – time, Cornford says that 'driven by a deep-lying need to master the world by understanding it, science works steadily toward its goal – a perfectly clear conceptual model of reality, adapted to explain all phenomena by the simplest formula that can be found ...' But Cornford saw that there's a catch. 'When we contemplate the finished result, we see that in banishing "the vague", it has swept away everything in which another type of mind finds all the value and significance of the world'.[23] That other type of mind is the spirit of finesse, the intuitive approach, Jünger's 'master key', the glance that takes in everything, all at once, and not bit by bit, one step at a time.

Banishing 'the vague' may seem like a good idea. Of course we want things to be clear, simple, and direct, and that is something the left brain, according to McGilchrist, is very good at making them. But too much clarity can obscure things as well as reveal them. The sun's light hides the stars. A 'perfectly clear conceptual model of reality, adapted to explain all phenomena by the simplest formula' sounds like the most 'cost efficient' way of explaining the world and ourselves. But efficiency isn't everything and 'the vague' for Cornford means the kinds of things amenable to Pascal's spirit of finesse, but not his spirit of geometry. It means values like beauty, freedom, love, things that are important in a more than utilitarian way, whose importance is in themselves and not as a means to some practical or socially beneficial end. They are, as George Steiner calls them, 'the sovereignly useless'.[24] They are not good *for* anything, however thinkers of a Darwinian slant may say they are. They give life meaning and are what make it worth living. When Jesus said that man does not live by bread alone, this is what he had in mind.

What happens when a reasonable desire for a 'clear conceptual model of reality' arrived at by 'the simplest formula that can be found,' gets out of hand? Scientism happens, which is successful precisely because it *reduces* reality to what it can abstract from it and apply to useful ends. We tend to associate reductive science with matter and materialism. But 'matter' itself is an abstraction. It is not the stuff we encounter in the world, but our *conceptual* grasp of it. We have all seen material things – they surround us – but no one has ever seen matter.[25] What is wrong with Scientism is not that it is 'material' but that it is too *abstract*, too much in love with the hunt for the simplest formula, which today takes the form of a 'theory of everything'. To be effective science must limit the part of reality that it deals with to what is relevant for its purposes. Because of this, as Barzun tells us, 'the realm of abstraction, useful and far from unreal, is thinner and barer and poorer than the world it is drawn from'.[26]

To abstract means to 'extract' or 'remove' something, whether it is an 'abstract' of a scientific paper you are interested in – that is, a brief description of it – or your idea of 'tree' from all the many, different 'real' trees you have encountered. One of the great sleights of hand that Scientism has pulled off is to convince the unthinking public that the thin, bare, poor world that it *abstracts* from – i.e. 'pulls out of' – our thick, luxuriant, rich world is the 'really real' world, the one that 'objectively exists', while the one we encounter and love and struggle with is a kind of subjective illusion, housed within our individual island consciousness. It manages this trick solely because of the practical effectiveness it provides. Reducing reality to those parts of it that can be quantified and manipulated to our benefit ensured that the new way of knowing would quickly become the arbiter and guarantor or what was real and what was true. It worked, no doubt about that. But at a price.

So far we have looked, albeit briefly, at the development and success of one of the two traditions that Cornford argued were active at the dawn of our peculiarly Western mind. I say 'peculiarly Western' because, although it has spread around the globe, the kind of insatiable curiosity about the world – the desire to know what made it 'tick' and to apply this knowledge to practical ends – that arose among the Greeks in the Axial Age, seems not to have appeared elsewhere, or at least not in the same concentrated way. This is not to celebrate Eurocentrism, merely to recognise that Western consciousness has a particular task, which we can see as establishing and maintaining the creative polarity between our two traditions. And what is the other tradition?

As an example of the other tradition, Cornford points to Pythagoras, whom we've already spoken about. Although Thales preceded Pythagoras he was not in fact the first philosopher, if only because it was Pythagoras, who came some years after, who coined the word. He also contributed other important terms of our discussion: *cosmos*, for one, and *theōria*, which gives us our 'theory', for another. *Theōria* comes from the Greek *theōros*, which means 'spectator'. We still retain something of this root when we say we have a theory about something based on our 'speculation' about it. We can see Pythagoras as an early 'scientist' in the sense that he worked at arriving at a rational account of existence. We all know his theorem – or at least struggled to learn it in school – and his discovery of the octave, which is the basis of western music. But unlike Thales and his followers, Pythagoras did not think in terms of some fundamental stuff out of which the world was made.

As we've seen, he believed number was behind everything. That is, he thought in terms of a kind of principle, or idea, rather than some material substance. Pythagoras also saw philosophy as something more than rational inquiry, although it certainly was that. It was more like a religious or mystical discipline. We can say that with the Pythagorean Brotherhood, Pythagoras founded the first esoteric school, 'esoteric' being concerned with what is 'inner', either the 'inner' significance of a teaching or religion, or the shape of our 'inner' world. That is, it was a school aimed at not only a defensible conceptual model of reality, but at a change in consciousness, a change, that is, in the philosopher's inner world, his mind. This was the wisdom that the philosopher, the 'lover of wisdom', pursued.

Pythagoras began as a devotee of the Orphic mysteries, which were themselves a refinement of the earlier, more orgiastic rites of the drunken god Dionysus. The transgressive revels of Dionysus, and the more ascetic, meditative practices of the Orphics, had the same aim. They were concerned with awakening the spark of spiritual life that lay asleep, sunken in the 'portable tomb' of the body and its sense of itself as a separate, mortal individual. But while the Dionysiacs threw off the constraints of the conscious mind through wild excess, and the Orphics awakened the soul through denying the flesh, Pythagoras sought to raise the consciousness of his students – and himself – by the contemplation of the eternal principles of reality. Rather than escape the conscious mind (that kept one separated from the whole) or quieten the body (that drew one's awareness away from the soul) Pythagoras saw a different path. He saw that the spirit could be awakened – raised from the dead, as Orpheus, in the original myths, did his wife Eurydice – through philosophy.[27] This meant achieving a harmony within oneself that matched the cosmic harmony without, what he, or his followers, called 'the music of the spheres'.

Pythagoras sought to achieve a creative balance between the older, mythical kind of consciousness, embodied in the Dionysian and Orphic mysteries, and the newer, mental one. In fact 'harmony', with which Pythagoras is associated, means 'balance', achieving a good 'fit'. Such a balance is difficult to reach, but attempts to achieve it are not infrequent in the history of Western consciousness, nor are successes unknown. As Barzun points out, Pascal himself is 'proof that one can be a great geometer and a profound intuiter'. (We've seen that McGilchrist, too, is in both camps.) Barzun optimistically suggests that 'any good mind properly taught can think like Euclid and like Walt Whitman'.[28]

It is not a question of two species of individual, or of 'two cultures', as a book by C.P. Snow, himself a scientist and a novelist, argued in the 1950s. The notion of two separate cultures or two 'kinds' of mutually exclusive minds – not two ways of using one mind – is a product of the proliferation of specialisation, first within the sciences, and then, in imitation of them, within the humanities (or 'social sciences', something, I think, of a misnomer) themselves. It is not the case that a vague, implicit mind can't handle clear conceptual models, or that minds attuned to the simplest formula can't stomach intuitions, although in individual cases the ability to do so, of course, varies. It is the information explosion that has been going on for some time now that keeps not only the two cultures separate from each other; it also separates scientists from scientists and literary critics from their fellows too. The sheer amount of material produced in each niche makes it impossible to keep up with anything outside of them, and the niches themselves are on the increase. Scientists may not talk to poets, but they also don't speak with many other scientists, outside their speciality, either. The problem here is not that of two cultures not understanding each other, but of too much information – most of it, as the policy of 'publish or perish' ensures, of dubious quality.

We can say that the other tradition that followed the Pythagorean approach – not necessarily his teachings – aims to achieve a kind of creative polarity between our two ways of knowing. It recognises the value of the new, quantitative way, the spirit of geometry. But it also recognises the value of the other way, the spirit of finesse. It also recognises that when the two are brought together in a creative tension something greater than either one can emerge. When the vague, implicit meanings are unpacked by an articulate mind attuned to them, and when the abstractions needed to conceptualise reality are informed by a wider, overall sense of context, then something that we might call genius, or at least insight, can occur. The other tradition does not want to jettison its mythic, intuitive heritage in its eagerness to explain the world in some eloquent, economical way. Nor does it want to plunge back into the warm waters of our earlier mode of consciousness, enjoying an inarticulate sense of connection to the All, something with which it is often confused. It also does not want to alleviate the tensions that arise out of the opposition between the two ways of knowing by way of some bland, placid compromise, a lukewarm agreement between hot and cold. It wants, as I've said elsewhere, to reach that Goldilocks moment, when the balance between the two is 'just right'.

There is, of course, no formula for this. If there were we would all have achieved it by now – notwithstanding some attempts to pin it down and get 'genius in a bottle'. But given that we have been working under the edicts of the new way of knowing for some centuries now, it seems to me, and to others, that we may need a refresher course in our other way of knowing. It has never gone away, even though periodically pontiffs of Scientism declare that it was ever only a misunderstanding and muddle of what is now absolutely clear, and that it has henceforth departed – only to appear again shortly after. This tradition, however, while a part of our heritage – because it is part of ourselves – is by its nature fluid and shifting, and less easily and clearly defined than its rival. As we've seen, it does not operate with fixed, exact definitions and unchanging sequential orders or algorithms, but with patterns, relationships, sympathies, analogies, intuitions, insights, and a synoptic grasp of experience – that is, it takes it in 'at a glance'.

Elsewhere I write about our other way of knowing in the context of a history of the Western esoteric tradition, the body of inner, mystical, or occult knowledge that has come down to us from ancient sources such as Hermetism, Gnosticism, Neoplatonism, Kabbalah, and also more recent ones.[29] The tradition this body of texts and practices represents is one, in the words of the historian of the occult James Webb, of 'rejected knowledge', a status it shares with the kind of intuitive knowledge and way of knowing I have been writing about here. It is rejected for the same reason that Jünger's 'master key' is, because it does not follow the prescribed rules of what 'real' knowledge should be like. There is also, as Jünger points out, a kind of professional jealousy. Those with the master key to the 'house of intellect' – a nod to a once influential book by Barzun – 'penetrate effortlessly into the single rooms, arousing the wrath of the specialists who watch their banks of files invalidated at a single stroke'.[30] If we can find our way out of the maze with one step, without a map, we will soon put the cartographers out of business.

The watchdogs of geometry do not care for the inexplicable bull's-eyes of their rivals, and generally do their best to disparage them or to explain them away in terms of their own ideas. That, in fact, is one of the themes I have explored elsewhere: namely that the Western esoteric tradition, once held in high regard, has, since the arrival of the new way of knowing, been subject to the kind of left brain aggression that, McGilchrist argues, the right brain has been enduring for some time now.[31] I see the Western esoteric tradition as a body of what we might call 'right brain knowledge'. And although it certainly had its troubles with religious dogma, both from the Church and, later, Islam, it was not until the arrival of the new quantitative way of knowing that it completely fell from grace and was relegated to the dustbin of ideas. But just as our other way of knowing has never been and cannot be excised from ourselves – without, I believe, fatal consequences – our tradition of 'rejected knowledge' has never truly disappeared. It has emerged in different ways at different times and in different places, reminding those aware of it that a different way of knowing ourselves and our world, that does not reduce it to the 'simplest formula to be found', exists, and is there to help us be 'fully human'.

Some of this rejected knowledge and the people who pursued it will appear in the pages that follow. As mentioned, one of the difficulties in speaking about this other tradition is the simple one of what to call it, given that, by definition it is not something to which clear definitions apply. This is something that hamstrings what we can call the various 'alternative' approaches to life, society, Nature, and so on, that have grown up over the last half a century or so, and which are generally, and erroneously I believe, corralled under the heading 'New Age' or 'New Science' or some other misleading, unedifying title. We simply don't have a good name to give it, that can cover all its aspects adequately, and also give an interested party something solid to hold onto. This is also because it is not so much a 'new' age or 'new' science, but a *different* way of looking at the age and science we already have. We are not necessarily looking for new facts, but for a new way of looking at the facts we already know.

Another reason for the ambiguity is that it is generally the established tradition that does the naming, and as it is not exactly in sympathy with the concerns of its alternative, it will not necessarily be very accurate in what it calls it. Another reason is the wide variety of different ideas, teachings, practices, and beliefs that are lumped together by virtue of their being 'other' than the dominant ones. This can lead to some confusion and odd pairings, with books on UFOs, Satanism, diet, or health, being put in the same category as those on Western esotericism, mysticism, or philosophies of consciousness. This is not to disparage aliens, Satanists, or people concerned about the spiritual dimensions of their diet. But it does mean that serious students of esoteric philosophy often have to devote considerable time to explaining the difference between their pursuits and these others, when asked exactly what esotericism is about.

While I was writing *The Secret Teachers of the Western World,* a phrase kept returning to me with an insistence that forced me to pay attention to it. It was coined by the poet, essayist, and Blake scholar Kathleen Raine. Raine, who I met on a few occasions and interviewed some years ago, spoke of what she called 'the lost knowledge of the imagination'.[32] This was linked to something she called 'the learning of the imagination', a phrase that she found in the work of the poet W.B. Yeats, himself a devotee, as was Raine, of the tradition of 'rejected knowledge'. A 'lost knowledge' and a 'rejected knowledge' – Raine also speaks of an 'excluded knowledge' – may not be identical, but they certainly seem rather similar, and in the great dustbin of ideas, filled to the brim by the rigorous editing of the new way of knowledge, they must, I suspect, be close neighbours.

Raine wrote many books arguing that this 'lost' or 'excluded' knowledge was in fact central to our humanity, and in them she showed how some of the most respected figures in Western culture were in fact students of it. She even went so far as to establish an academy dedicated to this knowledge, which she christened *Temenos,* a Greek word meaning 'sacred space', the holy ground that lay before a temple to the gods. Like William Blake, Raine laboured at this 'mental fight' for many years, dedicating her life to it. She died in 2003 at the age of ninety-five.

This book is about this 'lost' knowledge of the imagination. Yet, while this may give us a handy phrase under which we can put examples of the other kind of knowing I have been speaking about, it is not immediately clear what we mean by 'imagination'. Imagination is one of those things which we all know intimately but which we would find difficult to pin down exactly. It is one of those things that, as Whitehead said, are 'incapable of analysis in terms of factors more far-reaching than themselves'.[33] That is to say, we can't get 'under' imagination because the very act of trying to do so requires imagination itself. Memory, self-consciousness, thought, perception: all inform and are informed by imagination and are difficult, if not impossible, to pry apart from it or each other. This should not be surprising. Imagination does not follow the clear axioms and definitions of the spirit of geometry, but the wayward, vague, surprising insights of the spirit of finesse. As Blake himself said, 'Improvement makes straight roads, but the crooked roads, without Improvement, are roads of Genius'.[34] In the pages ahead of us, we will follow some of these crooked roads of genius, and see where they will lead us.

There are of course many books on the imagination. Psychological studies, motivational works, instructions in visualisation, research into creativity, guides to using imagination in business, relationships and self-improvement – these are some of the results that come from a quick internet search on the subject. There are many more. Most definitions of imagination speak of its contrast with reality. My *Oxford Dictionary* tells me that imagination is the 'mental faculty of forming images or concepts of objects or situations not existent or not directly experienced'. *Merriam-Webster* tells me it is 'the ability to imagine things that are not real' – which seems something of a tautology – and 'something that only exists or happens in your mind'. The *Cambridge Dictionary* says that imagination is 'the ability to form pictures in the mind' and that it concerns 'something that you think exists or is true, although in fact is not real or true'. Imagination is of course also creative. *Roget's Thesaurus* calls it the 'power to create in one's mind,' and samples of the synonyms it provides range from 'artistry,' 'awareness,' and 'inspiration', to 'ingenuity,' 'insight' and 'creativity'.

I believe imagination is one of those things which we all know immediately but which, as I've said, we would find difficult to define. Indeed, an exact definition of it would only make it more obscure.[35] Nevertheless, here I will offer my own definition of imagination. It is not necessarily exclusive of others; I give it to emphasise what I take to be imagination's central work, and also to make clear how it is a different way of understanding the imagination. I take it from Colin Wilson, who in his own work explored the evolutionary potential of imagination. Imagination, he said, is 'the ability to grasp realities that are not immediately present'. Not an escape from reality, or a substitute for it, but a deeper engagement with it. We could also say that imagination is simply our ability to grasp reality, or even, in some strange way, to create it, or at least to collaborate in its creation. For the moment let us limit ourselves to the first formulation.

It is because we need imagination to grasp reality – that part of it immediately before us, and its wider horizons that exceed the reach of our physical senses – that we can speak of a 'knowledge' of the imagination. Imagination has a noetic character; it is the source and medium of our other way of knowing. It shows us aspects and dimensions of reality that we would miss without it – and which much, if not most of official Western culture has missed since the new way of knowing became dominant. While it can be used for fantasy, illusion, make-believe, and escapism, the real work of imagination is to make contact with the strange world in which we live and to serve as both guide and inspiration for our development within it. It is the way we evolve. Imagination presents us with possible, potential realities that it is our job to actualise. It also presents us with a world that would not be complete without our help.

Let us look then for this lost knowledge of the imagination, and see how much of it we can find.

Chapter Two
A Look Inside the World

When we open our eyes we see before us a world that we naturally assume would be there whether we were or not. It is a world that exists 'outside' us, an 'objective' world, as we say, of solid, independent, discrete 'objects' or 'things' laid out in what we call 'space' and happening in what we call 'time'. Some of these things we see make up what we call 'Nature': trees, clouds, mountains, stars, rivers, oceans, valleys. We know that something along these lines most likely exists in other areas of space and did exist at other points of time, and we assume that they will exist in the future. We have yet to find life on any other planet, and what we have learned about the planets closest to us makes them sound rather inhospitable. But while we might not find trees or rivers or cities on the surface of Mars, whatever we do find there, or anywhere else, will exist, just as what we encounter here on Earth does, 'outside' us.

Some of the things we see are living – plant life, animals, and other people like ourselves. Indeed, for someone else, *we* are 'objectively there', just as they are for us – something it may take an effort of imagination to grasp. And some of the things we see, perhaps most these days, are 'man made'. They are not 'natural' and only came into existence through the work of human beings. The cities we live in, the airplanes overhead, the cars we drive in and the roads they follow, the computer I am writing this on and the television I will watch later this evening: these, and many other things too obvious to mention, are the result of human effort.

All this seems clear and, as I say, too obvious to point out. We assume that this is the natural, given, normal way of things and that something like this must have always been the case. The philosopher Edmund Husserl called seeing the world in this way 'the natural standpoint'. We really can't help it. We seem to be made this way. The world as I see it existed before I came on the scene and it will be here after I depart, and my entrance and exit will do little to change it.

In fact, according to the natural standpoint, the world was here before *anyone* turned up and it will remain after the last flicker of consciousness, human or otherwise, dies out. When the first humans became self-conscious and gazed out on the world, we assume they saw it in the same way that we do, as something 'outside' them. There were no buildings, no cities, no shopping malls, no highways or airports. Our man-made world did not exist. But the natural world did, and the humans who were waking up to that world experienced it in much the same way as we do today. We know a great deal more about the world than our ancestors did, in the sense of our new way of knowing, and this knowledge is what sets us apart from them. It's what constitutes our 'progress'. But the world our prehistoric ancestors experienced and the one we do today are the same. We just understand it better than they did.

This is the conventional picture of our relationship *vis-à-vis* the world and its past and it is one that most of us do not question. We see no reason to question it as it seems too obvious to doubt. Some people do question it, and depending on how they express their doubts we call them poets, or philosophers, or mystics, or madmen; Husserl, whom we've mentioned, was one of them. We will return to them shortly; for the most part they make an exception to the rule and in any case, no one pays much attention to them. The general consensus remains. There is the world outside, and there is me, or at least my consciousness, 'inside' my head, just as there is your consciousness inside yours.

I say that at least my consciousness is 'inside my head' because, as mentioned, the head in which my consciousness is supposed to reside is, as the rest of my body is, a part of the 'outside' world. It is part of the outside world to other people, but strangely it is also part of the outside world to me. I can see my head in a mirror and hold it in my hands, but I can't see my inside or touch it in any way.[1] I can, in the interests of science, allow my head to be opened and its interior inspected. The strange thing here is that the 'inside' that I believe is there, and which I experience all the time, won't be found. What the scientists examining me will find is my brain, a soggy lump of densely convoluted organic matter weighing about three pounds, the work of whose different hemispheres we discussed in the last chapter. If, in the further interest of science, I allow this mass of grey matter to be opened as well, my inside will still not be found. This has led many prestigious people to declare that the inside I am looking for doesn't really exist. It is an illusion somehow created by the physical processes taking place in my brain, whether the neurochemical exchanges going on between its synapses, or something further down, at the molecular or sub-atomic level.[2] In any case it is an 'outside' phenomenon that somehow gives rise to my experiencing an 'inside'.[3]

My inside is the only one I know directly, the only one of which I have any immediate experience. I assume that the other people I see when I look out into the world have an inside much like my own, but I cannot know this directly. Yet I must assume that their inside is more or less like mine; for one thing, life would be very difficult if I didn't. Our inner furnishings may differ – we all have different ideas, memories, fantasies, thoughts – but the general floorplan of our interiors must be the same.

We can say that each of our own independent 'insides' consists of two parts. This is of course an oversimplification but for our immediate purposes here it will serve. We can say that one part of our inside is a kind of mirror with a sort of camera attachment, that reflects the world and also takes snapshots of it. The other part is a storeroom where I keep the pictures. This in a nutshell is the picture of our inside, our consciousness, that has been accepted since the philosopher René Descartes first proposed something like it in his *Meditations on First Philosophy,* published in 1641. It has certainly been dominant since John Locke, who followed Descartes, argued that there 'is nothing in the mind that was not first in the senses', as he did in his *Essay On Human Understanding,* published in 1689. Both works appeared in the early days of our new way of knowing, and in fact were instrumental in establishing it. Locke actually disagreed with Descartes. Descartes believed that our storeroom contained some items that were there before we started taking photographs. He called these 'innate ideas'. Locke didn't believe in innate ideas, but the disagreement he had with Descartes is less important here than what they had in common.

According to Locke and philosophers like David Hume who came after him, our inside is empty until we start taking pictures and putting them in the storeroom, rather like a new flat is empty until we go to Ikea and fill it up with stuff, or a mirror is blank until we put something in front of it.[4] I can reach into this storeroom and find some of the photographs I've taken. This is called memory. Most of the time, these photographs float around as it were, and come to me – whoever that is – unbidden, often when I don't want them. But when I do I can retrieve some of them, even if they are not as vivid or clear as when I first took them. And I can move the photographs around and even cut them up and rearrange them, as an artist makes a collage. This produces something 'new', in the sense that what I arrive at wasn't originally photographed in that form. But it is made up of things that I did originally photograph. So it is not so much new content, but a new or different arrangement of old content.

As we will see, this is the distinction that the poet Samuel Taylor Coleridge made between fantasy and imagination, with fantasy doing collage work, and imagination creating something that is truly 'new'. For Coleridge a unicorn or a flying pig is a product of fantasy, of putting together different bits and pieces of our snapshots. True imagination is something else. But if Locke is right, then it is difficult to see how we can have anything other than fantasy, a point we will return to.

In his attempt to secure some indubitable nugget of certainty, necessary for us to truly understand the world, Descartes arrived at his famous formula, *Cogito ergo sum:* he thought, therefore he was. While he could doubt everything else in his experience as possibly an illusion created by some demon, he could not doubt his own existence, for in order to be tricked by a demon, he would have to exist. For Descartes this provided an Archimedean point from which he could erect a new model of the universe, or at least of our experience of it, and we honour him by coupling his name with Newton's as one of the creators of the modern world.

Descartes secured his certainty, at least to his own satisfaction, but at a price. The cost was the split between mind and matter, or more immediately, mind and body, our inside and outside, that has hampered human understanding ever since. After much meditation Descartes decided that there were two fundamental kinds of things in reality, or in fact two realities, what he called *res cogitans* and *res extensa,* 'thinking' or 'knowing' things, and 'extended' things. This was the knowing mind and what it knows, or, in our terms here, our inside and the outside, consciousness and the external world.

We need not follow Descarte's argument; his conclusion is what matters. It matters because there seemed to be no clear, comprehensible way that these two different things could 'interact', as we say – a problem neuroscientists and philosophers of mind still encounter when they consider how one gets from a neuron, which is physical, to a thought, which is not, what is known as the 'hard problem'.

Descartes believed that the two realities did interact – they had to, as we experienced this in ourselves all the time – and he thought that this happened in a tiny organ in the brain called the pineal gland. This is located behind the third ventricle and strangely, this is also where in ancient Hindu tradition the 'third eye' is found, the 'opening' of which triggers mystical vision.[5] Descartes laboured hard to find a way for the two realities to get together there, but ultimately he did not manage it. The task was taken up by others, notably the eighteenth century Swedish scientist and religious philosopher Emanuel Swedenborg, although he too eventually gave it up.[6] It was in fact Swedenborg's failure to find 'the seat of the soul' in the brain that led to his abandoning science and the beginning of what we can call his 'visionary' period, during which he made several visits to heaven, hell and an intermediary sphere he called the spirit world.[7] More on this later.

Descartes' failure to find the 'seat of the soul' and his method of radical doubt started what Colin Wilson called a 'forest fire' in Western philosophy that ended by 'consuming everything', a catastrophe from which philosophy is still recovering.[8] One thing Descartes' blaze did eventually consume was our 'inside'. In a way this made sense, as he had already got rid of an inside to everything else. The outer world, for him, was really just a machine, moved by purely physical forces; even animals were really only machines, or what we would call robots. They only appeared to suffer pain or to express emotions; in reality they were empty mechanisms, moved solely by the push and pull of cause and effect. Our own bodies were subject to the same mechanical laws, but Descartes ring-fenced our subjectivity, our inside, protecting it temporarily from the fire he had started.

Others were less delicate. Through what seemed an irrevocable process, the *res cogitans* started to lose ground. This was inevitable, given the success of the new way of knowing, which recognised only 'objective', quantifiable, positively identifiable things that could be measured. Pascal's 'thinking reed' – his image of humankind – became a recording device, dependent on input from the outer world in order to function, a kind of 'penny in the slot' machine. Sensory input came in, and we responded accordingly. Eventually our inside became nothing more than a 'ghost in the machine', as the philosopher Gilbert Ryle famously called it in his book *The Concept of Mind,* and which Arthur Koestler used as the title of his book attacking the kind of reductive philosophy Ryle championed.

Since then many have tried to lay the ghost to rest, and I have written about some of their attempts elsewhere.[9] Many believe they have finally exorcised it. Yet many disagree, and dismiss the idea of a 'ghost' entirely, saying rather it is the machine that is unreal. One of these dissenters was the literary scholar and philosopher of language, Owen Barfield.

To those other than his many readers, Owen Barfield is perhaps best known as being the great friend of C.S. Lewis. He is also known to fans of J.R.R. Tolkien as being a member of the Inklings, the name given to a literary pub gathering in Oxford that included Tolkien, Lewis, and also Charles Williams, a Dante scholar, member of the Hermetic Order of the Golden Dawn, and author of some still readable 'esoteric thrillers'. Still others may know of Barfield through his writings about the philosophy of Rudolf Steiner. Barfield lived to the ripe age of ninety-nine; I met him in 1996, shortly before he died, and conducted what I believe was the last interview with him.[10]

Barfield began his career in 1926, with his first book *History in English Words.* His last, *History, Guilt, and Habit,* was published in 1981. In the intervening years Barfield wrote much else, including poetry and novels, but his theme remained the same. As he told me during our interview, he was what the philosopher Isaiah Berlin called a 'hedgehog,' who knows one big thing, in contrast with the 'fox', who knows many things. This was the reason why, he said, he had written the same book over and over for fifty years.[11] The one big thing that Barfield knew was what he called 'the evolution of consciousness', which he saw as 'the concept of man's self-consciousness as a process in time'.[12] And he had come to know this through a study of language.

Like imagination and consciousness, language seems to be one of those things that Whitehead said were 'incapable of analysis in terms of factors more far-reaching than themselves'. We may think we know how language 'works'. We must know, we believe, because we use it all the time. But when we try to spell this out explicitly, we quickly find ourselves confronting a mystery. Barfield expressed something of this difficulty when he said that 'asking about the origin of language is like asking about the origin of origin'.[13] In order to talk about imagination we must use imagination and in order to talk about language we must use language. We can't get behind them or stand apart from them, as detached observers, as we can with something in the physical world, but must understand them from 'inside'. That, in fact, is what Barfield set out to do.

Barfield's investigation into language began when he was a schoolboy. His Latin class was given an assignment in syntax and asked to analyse the sentence: *Cato, octoginta annos natus, excessit e vita.* A bare English translation is: 'Cato, eighty years of age, departed this life', meaning that he died. That would have been correct, but a schoolfriend of Barfield added some dash. 'Cato,' he said, 'at the age of eighty, *walked out of life.'* That, Barfield's friend said, was a 'rather nice' way of putting it.[14]

Barfield agreed. It was rather nice. In fact, it was more than nice. Putting it that way had a strange *living* character to it that conveyed more than the bare information that the great Roman historian died at the age of eighty. It added colour and movement, freshness and a kind of vitality. It was what we call 'figurative language', a metaphor, and at that moment Barfield first realised that one could enjoy metaphors and figures of speech – language itself in fact – for its own sake, and not only as a means of communicating something. Some years later Barfield found that the metaphors that he enjoyed most came from lyric poetry and the Romantic poets; that is, poetry about the poet's inner world, his feelings and emotions. As he said in a lecture he gave on the subject, these metaphors would bear 'not merely reading and enjoying'. There was something more to them. 'One could somehow dwell on them.' They altered the way in which he saw the world; it became 'a profounder and a more meaningful place when seen through eyes that had been reading poetry'. Poetry, he found, 'had the power to change one's consciousness a little'.[15] Exactly how it can change consciousness and why, was something Barfield was determined to understand.

Before I continue I should perhaps make clear what a metaphor is. Like language and imagination, metaphors are something we use all the time but rarely notice, unless, like Barfield, we have a keen ear or eye for them. My *Oxford Dictionary* tells me that a metaphor is 'the application of a name or description to something to which it is not literally applicable'. The *Cambridge Dictionary* tells me it is 'an expression, often found in literature, that describes a person or object by referring to something that is considered to have similar characteristics to that person or object'. Other sources give similar definitions.

We can say that a metaphor is something that stands for, or takes the place of, something else, to which it is related, but not in an obvious way. It is something more than a sign. A sign is merely an indicator, pointing toward something. It does not add to our understanding of it. A metaphor points to what it stands for, but it also brings out or allows more 'meaning' to emerge from its subject, a meaning that is in addition to the bare information it provides. In this way it is more like a symbol, which can have multiple meanings, than a sign which has only one.

Literalness, we can say, is using language solely with its exact, explicit meaning and nothing else. It is a very 'left brain' way of speaking; the left brain has a difficult time with metaphors but for the right they aren't a problem. If you told a very literal person that a friend was so happy that he was 'over the moon', he would very likely say: 'That's impossible. Where did he get the rocket from?' For a literal person a rose is a rose is a rose and nothing else. For a person with a metaphorical mind a rose can be many things.

If you told a very literal person that someone exploded with anger, he would look for the pieces. If you told him a pretty woman's face bloomed, he would look for the petals.

Many science fiction stories have scenes in which a robot or android or some other very 'logical' individual – think of *Star Trek's* Mr Spock – is at a loss to understand the metaphorical speech of humans. These scenes aim to elicit some humour in the contrast between the 'cold' logic of the robot and the 'warm' feeling of the humans. But we can do the same thing whenever we point to metaphors that we use regularly but no longer recognise as metaphors. They have hardened, as it were, into stock phrases, whose figurative character no longer makes an impact, the kind of impression young Barfield felt when hearing of Cato 'walking out of life'.

Much of our language is made up of these 'dead metaphors', and this has been pointed out by thinkers such as Emerson and Nietzsche. Emerson spoke of clichés as 'fossilised poetry' and Nietzsche used a metaphor himself, saying such words and phrases are like coins whose faces have been worn down by use. We have become so used to them that we forget that they once had a 'living' character. Barfield points this out using the phrase 'to leave no stone unturned', meaning an exhaustive search for something. Originally, it conveyed an image of someone flipping over stones with a pickaxe, but today we hardly think of this and recognise the phrase as a cliché. So, if in discussing some old affair, someone remarked that it was so long ago that it was 'water under the bridge', we could have a 'Mr Spock moment' by asking 'what bridge?' You get the picture? – which is, of course, only another metaphor.

This excursion into metaphor is important because metaphor plays a central role in Barfield's recognition that language provides evidence of an evolution of consciousness. Jumping ahead a bit we can say that for Barfield metaphor is a way of seeing the 'inside' of things, and not only their surface, which is what literal language limits itself to. Barfield will argue that, just as the metaphors we use harden over time and lose their living character, so too our language as a whole has gone through the same process. It started out as 'living' and able to express the inside of the world, and over time lost its vitality and became limited to only the surface of things.

What Barfield wants to say is that this has been the case because the way we *perceive* the world has changed over time, which means that our consciousness has changed. It has shifted, as the literary scholar Erich Heller said, from speaking poetry to speaking prose.[16]

At an earlier time, Barfield argues, humans perceived the world in a way that we today would say was very metaphorical, very figurative, and very poetical. We no longer see it that way, or do so only when stimulated by poetry, or if we alter our consciousness through some means, usually drugs or alcohol. Poetry and wine have long been linked, and they are fellow travellers because both can alter our perception of things. Both inspire the reflection that the world is more 'interesting' than we normally give it credit for being.

Barfield arrived at this insight by looking at the history of language. What he discovered, and spelled out in *History in English Language* and another early work, *Poetic Diction,* is that if we look back into the language of an earlier period, we see that it is more figurative than our own. This is why such early language can have the same effect on us as lyrical poetry has, of briefly showing us the world in a different way – in other words, changing our consciousness. As Barfield says: 'Almost any kind of language in fact that is expressing a consciousness essentially different from our own' can have this effect.[17] In lyric poetry the poet is consciously, or at least purposefully, aiming at creating striking metaphors that can convey the feelings, the inner experience, he wants to express. Living, figurative language is something he strives for. But in older language, the language of the past, this living character is simply there, in the language itself. It was not striven for, as the poet strives for it. It is just a part of language. The poet aims at altering our consciousness by using striking metaphors. The old language didn't aim at doing this, but it nevertheless did. Old language, Barfield saw, was doing by itself, what 'poetic language' aimed at doing intentionally.

The kinds of metaphor that made the strongest impression on Barfield, as they do on most readers of poetry, are the kinds that use a material image to express an immaterial idea. Barfield refers to the poet Shelley saying that the West Wind has made him its lyre.[18] What Shelley means is that he has been inspired by the wind to break out into song, not that he has been turned into an ancient musical instrument by it. A literal-minded person would have told Shelley that he didn't look at all like a lyre. The lyre is a material image that captures the immaterial change in Shelley's consciousness.

All of this got Barfield thinking about the roots of language and its relation to consciousness and to the world. Along with recognising that the further back we go in language, the more metaphorical and figurative it is, Barfield also saw, as other language philosophers have, that words today that have an abstract or immaterial content started out with more material origins. I spoke of Shelley being 'inspired' by the west wind. We think of inspiration as an immaterial thing, as a sudden impetus to creative activity. Yet 'inspire' is rooted in 'spirit' and means having the spirit put into you, while 'spirit' itself is rooted in a term for 'breath'.[19] We still acknowledge this root when we speak of alcohol as 'spirits', referring to the fumes given off by it. 'Impetus' itself, which we think of as 'motivation' has its roots in 'force' or 'energy', while motivation itself begins as that which gets us 'moving'. If you have 'grasped' what I have just written, that is a material image of a hand grabbing something, which we take as meaning we 'understand' it. 'Under/standing' itself is a material image of a mental process.

This idea, that our words for immaterial things started out as referring to material ones, led some nineteenth century language theorists to some important but questionable conclusions about its origins. Referring to what the philosopher Jeremy Bentham called our 'immaterial vocabulary' they said in effect that in the beginning 'immaterial meanings ... began their life ... by having purely material meanings, which were then extended by metaphor'.[20]

In other words, there were no 'real' immaterial things, then or now, just material things made to *seem* immaterial through the magic of metaphor.

What this seemed to say was that the language that we experience as figurative originally began as non-figurative, as, in other words, literal, and was then 'worked on', made figurative, and that is what we have inherited. From this point of view, all language in fact started in this way. Yet Barfield felt that this seemed not to chime with the evidence that language presents itself. This view suggested that language began as grunts and groans, either in an attempt to imitate natural sounds, or as a way of expressing surprise or some other emotion, what Barfield calls the 'bow wow' and 'ooh aah' theories. Out of these primitive sounds meaningful words were supposed to have arisen.

This seemed a common sense view, although the people espousing it failed to show how 'meaning' can have come from a consciousness that was assumed to be bereft of it, given that they more or less accepted John Locke's view of our 'inside'. It was assumed that grunts and groans were at some point transformed into meaningful words, designating material objects, that is, into literal language. Then at some point, a rash of 'prehistoric poets' got to work on this literal language and 'morphed' it into figurative language. Why they did this no one ever quite answered; we just have to assume a whole generation of ancient literary stylists simultaneously getting to work.

We have no record of this taking place, as the language that has come down to us arrived after this supposed 'age of metaphor'. Yet we must assume it happened. This was the only possible answer to the evidence language presented itself: that, as we've seen, the further back we go, the more metaphorical it is. Poking fun at the great Orientalist Max Müller, who can stand for the conventional language theorists he is questioning, Barfield writes that 'although when he moves backwards through the history of language, he [Müller] finds it becoming more and more *figurative* with every step, yet he has no hesitation in assuming a period – still further back – when it was not figurative at all!'[21] It is in order to account for this discrepancy that Müller and his fellow theorists have to call in a race of 'amateur poets' who, in the 'infancy of society', got to work churning out metaphors by the dozen.

But as Barfield knew, no one has drilled through the layers of metaphor that supposedly obscure our original non-figurative *Ur*-language and revealed this in all its primal literal glory. No matter how far back we go, we hit the wall of figurative language – literally.

Barfield realised that all of the theorists who held to this view started out with the same premise, an unvoiced one. In hindsight it seems inevitable that they should have done so; nevertheless, it has caused a great deal of confusion. The premise is the view of the world with which I began this chapter. They assumed, as we all do, that the world our prehistoric ancestors came to self-awareness in was exactly like the world we see today. Our man-made contributions to it were not, of course, available. But in all other regards it was the same. They saw the world, as we do, from Husserl's 'natural standpoint', as something 'outside', distinctly external to themselves. They saw it in the literal way that we do, when we are not speaking figuratively. For them a rose was a rose and nothing more – at least that's what it was after they came up with the name for it.

To this assumption the language theorists added another. As Barfield pointed out, this quest for the origin of language took place in a Darwinian climate. Evolution through natural selection was the rage, and Müller and other language theorists worked on the assumption that human consciousness had emerged from a purely animal one, from, that is, 'a consciousness to which any notion of meaning was inapplicable'. As Barfield writes:

> The human being, it was assumed, first awoke to self-awareness to find himself surrounded by a world of sharply defined objects; and that self-awareness gradually increased as he learned to control and manipulate these objects in the course of the struggle for existence, the struggle for survival.[22]

The most effective tool for his survival that early man hit upon was speech. So it was the pressure of having to survive that turned our prehistoric ancestors' grunts and groans into meaningful literal speech. Once that was settled, as we've seen, a cadre of poetical cavemen got to work inventing scores of metaphors, forever blocking our encounter with that primal matter-of-fact tongue.

It was practically impossible for the language theorists at the time to look at the situation in any other way. The unquestioned assumption that the trajectory that Darwin and his followers charted for human evolution was the obviously correct one compelled them to do so. How else could language have developed?

Barfield had some ideas about that. For the purposes of

speculation let us assume, he thought, that the prehistoric poets who turned the originally literal mother tongue into a metaphorical one, did not exist. Where does that leave us? For one thing, we would have to accept that, rather than starting out literal and then mysteriously being made metaphoric, language was metaphoric, that is figurative, to begin with. This would mean that our first speakers did not begin with matter-of-fact explicit designations for things, that later became figurative, but that their speech was figurative from the start. This would mean that it had the living, vital character that Barfield loved in lyric poetry and had discovered in older language.

Assuming this, what does it suggest? It suggested to Barfield that perhaps the world the first speakers were talking about was not like the world we see today – and again, not in the obvious way that there were mammoths in it rather than automobiles and lush virgin forests rather than car parks. Perhaps language began as figurative because the world itself then was more like how it is when we speak of it figuratively than how it is when we are being literal? This would mean that the first speakers spoke poetry, although they would not have thought of it this way. Poetry for us is a 'special' use of language, or at least it used to be, before the idea of poetry as either fractured prose or raw self-expression took hold sometime in the twentieth century. We have to go out of our way to write poetry, whereas prose, as Erich Heller observed, is our default setting for language.[23] The first speakers then would not have been poets as we understand them, but they would have seen the world and experienced it in a way that we today would consider 'poetical'. Speaking of the philosopher Hegel, who thought of the past as a 'fundamentally poetic state of the world', Erich Heller writes that this was a world:

> ... in which poetry is not merely written, but, as it were, lived. The active intervention and participation of gods in the lives of mortals; groves and springs and hills as the habitats of nymphs and fauns; the poetic comprehension of life was at that time not a matter of the poetic imagination at work in the minds of a few chosen individuals, of artists ... but was 'natural', a matter of fact, of ways of thinking and feeling shared by the whole community.[24]

'It is not absurd to say', Heller continues, 'that in such a world *our* distinctions between imagination and fact were of little importance, if not unknown'. Heller remarks that it was reflections like these that led a young Nietzsche 'to accuse the first great analytical rationalist of Greece, Socrates, the indefatigable questioner, of having destroyed mythology ...'[25]

We can say that the distinction between imagination and fact that Heller refers to as *ours,* started around the time of Jaspers' 'Axial Age' with the rise of rational thought and the move away from mythology. It achieved a kind of optimum form or apogee with Socrates and Plato (who still retained a good portion of the older mythological view), and then gradually began to atrophy; we can say that the hardening started with Aristotle. According to the philosopher Jean Gebser, it entered what he called its 'deficient mode' around the time of the Renaissance, and we can say that this reached a kind of manic intensity with the new way of knowing that appeared in the early seventeenth century and has dominated the Western mind ever since.[26] What we can see here, and what Barfield charts in his 'evolution of consciousness', is the gradual loss of an immediate awareness of the 'inside' of things, and our arrival at a point in which we doubt even the reality of the one inside we are sure of, or at least used to be – our own.

I don't think Barfield knew of Heller's work, or that Heller knew of his; at least I've not seen the one reference the other in any of their books. Yet both hit on the same idea: that our earliest perception and encounter with the world was one much more like poetry than prose, one that we would call much more 'imaginative' than how we see the world today. Yet, as Heller says, echoing Barfield, it is a mistake to give the credit for this to the poetic imagination of a few individuals. No one 'made' it that way. It was 'natural', 'matter of fact', and shared by entire communities. And here we have a neat turnaround.

As we have noted, early language theorists say that our speech started out as literal, as matter of fact, and then somehow became poetic. Heller is saying: 'No, it started out poetic, but such poetic language was "matter of fact" for the people at the time, and it then only gradually became prosaic'. I turn to my *Oxford Dictionary* and I find that 'matter-of-fact' means 'unimaginative, prosaic, unemotional'. Other definitions include 'dry', 'commonplace', 'straightforward', 'down-to-earth', 'everyday'. So what we seem to have here is a way of being in the world that to us would seem 'imaginative' but which to the people experiencing it would seem 'business as usual'. They saw the world in a way very different from our own, but to them it was 'normal'.

What was their 'normal'? If the figurative character, what Barfield calls the 'presence of living imagery', that we find in early language was not 'made', as it is today by poets (those, of course, still writing true poetry), how did it come about? Barfield says it was just there in the language. It was a given kind of meaning, a given kind of imagery, just as the static, literal world we see from the 'natural standpoint' is given to us when we open our eyes. And if this living imagery was 'given' – was 'the case', as the philosopher Wittgenstein may have put it – along with the 'imaginal meaning in the earliest words', one wants to ask *who* gave it?[27]

'There must have been going on,' Barfield says, 'not only a different kind of thinking but a different kind of perceiving'. He continues: 'the picture quality, the given meanings must have been present not only in the perceiver but also in what he perceived; *it must have been present in fact in the world around him*' [my italics]. Barfield then goes on to make his central point, a very important part of his 'one big thing'. 'There must have been,' he says, 'a kind of participation between perceiver and perceived, between man and nature'. This means that we must envision a kind of world in which the strict separation of inside and outside, subjective and objective, living and dead, fact and imagination that we experience was not the case.

We no longer experience this, Barfield acknowledges, except for the brief tastes of it we have through our imagination. I would add to this that a determined attempt to completely exorcise 'participation' from our consciousness began with the rise of our new way of knowing in the seventeenth century.[28] But we can get a glimpse of it, as Barfield says, 'through the creative imagination of a modern painter or poet'.[29] To this list we can also add the use of certain substances whose effect, I would argue, is to put our consciousness back into this earlier, participatory state. I mentioned wine earlier; that there are more powerful and risky substances is common knowledge today. Poetry and art may be less immediately powerful than these, but their use, as it were, is wholly beneficial, and the change they bring about longer lasting.

Barfield contends that language emerged from this 'participation' and could be best described at its beginning as 'nature speaking through man, rather than man speaking about nature'.[30] Man then was 'spoken into being before he himself began to speak', a phrase that is reminiscent of the philosopher Heidegger's remarks that 'language is the house of being' and that 'language speaks man', rather than the other way around.[31] Language developed, according to Barfield, because what he calls 'original participation' dwindled over time. This evolution of language, Barfield believes, took the 'form of a contraction of meaning and therefore of consciousness – an evolution from wide and vague to narrow and precise, and from what was peripherally based to what is centrally based'.[32] Elsewhere Barfield speaks of a shift from a 'vague but immediate awareness of the "meaning" of phenomena' – that is, nature – 'towards an increasing preoccupation with the phenomena themselves,' and of a 'contraction of human consciousness from periphery to centre – a contraction from the cosmos of wisdom to something like a purely brain activity'.[33] In terms of language, this is the shift from a figurative, poetic kind of speech to a prosaic one.

This shift from the 'wide and vague' to the 'narrow and precise' seems similar to the shift from a right brain way of knowing to a left brain one that we remarked on in the previous chapter. It also suggests a movement from a metaphorical thinking to a more literal kind and reminds us once again of what was said earlier about the 'two permanent needs of human nature'.

What it also suggested to Barfield is that it is meaningless to ask about the 'origin' of language, at least in the way that early language theorists thought of this. They thought of language appearing in a world already 'there', a world like the one they themselves inhabited. As we've seen, Barfield says this is wrong. Language did not appear at some point in a world already given; language and 'the world' that we know emerged simultaneously as two separate phenomena as a result of the loss of original participation, that is of a prior unity encompassing both. And that loss of original participation itself resulted in the polarity of inner and outer worlds that we experience today. Consciousness, from being spread out and interfused – as Wordsworth would say – with its world began to contract, to become more definite by becoming more limited, finding its home more and more within the confines of our skulls.[34] As Barfield writes in *Saving the Appearances,* in original participation 'man was a part of nature in a way which we today … find it difficult to conceive'. What nascent sense of self there was knew that 'it and the phenomena' – that is, the natural world – came from what Barfield calls the 'same supersensible source'. It was aware of its link to its surroundings through an inner sense, not the outer ones. Man's soul, Barfield says, was not yet his own, meaning that his inside was not yet his 'private property' as it appears to be for us. As Barfield writes, the further back we go, the 'more indistinguishable' would human 'acts and utterances become from processes taking place in what has since become "outer" nature'.[35]

Slowly, Barfield says, the human psyche 'gradually drew forth its own meaning from the meaning of its environment'. It began to separate itself and it was in this process that the polarity 'man' and 'world' came into being.[36] So, from this point of view, there was no 'origin of language' separate from an 'origin of the world' and 'origin of man'. All three were part of the same evolution. This is why Barfield says that looking for the origin of language is like looking for the origin of origin.[37] 'Speech did not arise as the attempt of man to imitate, to master or to explain "nature"', Barfield says. 'Speech and nature came into being along with one another'.[38] There was no world separate from ourselves until language could speak it.

Many have bemoaned the loss of this Adamic speech, the *Ursprache* spoken in Eden, with which Man gave names to God's creation, when word and world were one. And the change in consciousness that so delighted Barfield as he read the Romantic poets was precisely a return of this lost participation, coupled with the awareness of self that was gained by its loss. He 'participated' but he also *knew* that he did. This is what in *Saving the Appearances* Barfield calls 'final participation'. That is to say, the flash of 'meaning' that lyric poetry produces, is not so much a plunge back into our earlier unconscious participation, but a conscious grasp of it – a conscious *experience* of it – brought about by 'mental activity', that of the poet and the reader; that is, through their imagination.[39] This produces an 'expansion' of meaning rather than its 'contraction,' which is the result of the drift into a literal way of seeing the world.[40] It is a moment of what Colin Wilson calls 'duo-consciousness', and which Barfield, following Coleridge, calls 'polarity'.[41]

Barfield does not see our exit from Eden as a 'fall' so much as a necessary sacrifice in order to achieve self-consciousness. What has happened though, is that what began as a necessary polarisation into an inside and outside has, with the new way of knowing appearing in the seventeenth century, become an 'exclusive disjunction'. The polarisation of inner and outer, necessary for human self-consciousness, has now widened into a true rift, what Whitehead called a 'bifurcation', meaning a division. And as we've seen, this had led many to doubt the existence of our inside at all. The outer, phenomenal world, with which at some unconscious source we are joined, has become for us a completely alien 'other'. By forgetting its unity with ourselves we have turned it, as Barfield says, into an 'idol'. And we have so succumbed to our 'idolatry' that rather than understand the world in terms of our consciousness – which for Barfield are *pari passu,* two sides of the same thing – we work diligently to explain consciousness in terms of the world; that is, to explain our inside in terms of the outside. This, for Barfield, is like trying to explain the origin of language in the way that the earlier language theorists did, with a world quite like ours in which primitive man was prodded by his physical needs to turn grunts and groans into words and then to quickly work some metaphorical magic on them. For them, there is only a physical world 'out there' that, in some still inexplicable but soon to be clarified way, gave rise to our illusory world 'in here'.

But Barfield saw that a vivid grasp of both our own inside and that of the world can be had through figurative language. This, as he says, allows us to see through one meaning of a word to another. It is this translucence that allows for the vaguer, indefinite, implicit meaning of things to be conveyed, what Barfield sees as an inner meaning arising from an outer one.[42] Literalism, precisely the lack of imagination, wants to contend that the monotone opaque way in which it presents the world, showing only its surface, is the truth. But as Barfield points out, such literalism is the end product of an historical process, the shift from a poetic way of seeing the world to a prosaic one. Its success depends on it purposefully ignoring a dimension of reality, its depth and inwardness.

We can regain a sense of participation today, but it costs a certain effort. Meaning, Barfield tells us, cannot be conveyed directly from one person to another; 'words', he says, 'are not bottles.' But we can intuit meaning for ourselves, if we make a certain kind of effort, what Barfield calls a 'special exertion' of the imagination.

In the last chapter I spoke of a kind of imaginative knowledge that the German writer Ernst Jünger described as a master key, that enables one to go to the heart of the problem immediately. Jünger calls the act of doing this 'stereoscopy', a kind of double vision in which surface and depth are perceived simultaneously.[43] He says its 'action consists in grasping things with our inner claws'.[44] 'True language, the language of poets,' Jünger writes, 'is distinguished through words and images that are seized in this manner'. Such words, 'although they are long familiar to us, unfold like flowers and appear to radiate an immaculate luster, a colourful music', what Jünger calls a 'secret harmony'.[45]

Such double vision, Jünger believes, allows us to overcome the dichotomy between 'the surface of life and its depths'.[46] As it is now we move from one to the other – we can say from science to poetry – without being able to bring the two together. Often the depths seem merely the means of creating the glittering surface, which we find beautiful and fascinating – Jünger himself was a keen entomologist, and a species of beetle that he discovered is named after him. But at other times the surface seems 'composed only of signs and letters, through which the depths speak to us of their secrets'.[47] Jünger reflects that in a crystal, surface and depth appear simultaneously to the eye (we are reminded of Barfield's use of the work 'translucent'). A crystal, he says, can 'generate inner surfaces' and can 'turn its depth outwards,' and Jünger wonders if the world itself is like a crystal, even if we perceive it in this way only seldom.[48]

Elsewhere I have written about the work of the eccentric French

Egyptologist and alchemist, René Schwaller de Lubicz.[49] In his own way and through a different route, Schwaller de Lubicz hit upon an insight that I relate to Barfield's ideas about language and 'participation'. Schwaller spent years studying the Great Pyramid, the monuments at Luxor and Karnak, and other ancient sites, and he came to believe that their main purpose was to serve as compendia of esoteric knowledge, the kind of knowledge that was resolutely rejected by the West in the seventeenth century. The ancient Egyptians had access to this knowledge through what Schwaller called 'the intelligence of the heart'. In essence, like Barfield's 'participation', the intelligence of the heart allowed the Egyptians – or at least their high priests and those who designed their monuments – to see into the 'inside' of the world. What they saw there was a 'cosmic harmony', the balancing of the spiritual forces at work creating and maintaining the universe.

Through the 'intelligence of the heart' Schwaller believed that the Egyptians could participate with these forces. As he wrote in his oracular posthumous work *Nature Word* – the title itself suggests a link to Barfield – with the intelligence of the heart we can 'tumble with the rock that falls from the mountain', 'seek light and rejoice with the rosebud about to open', and 'expand in space with the ripening fruit'.[50] All of this, it seems to me, sounds very much like a world in which figurative language was the norm.

The Egyptians saw the world symbolically, Schwaller believed; for them it was a kind of text to be interpreted. They were able to 'read' the world in this way through what Schwaller called *symbolique*. For him this meant an ability to hold different, sometimes contradictory ideas together simultaneously – something rather similar to Jünger's 'stereoscopy'. The hieroglyph of a bird stood for the animal; that was its 'outer' meaning. But it also had another meaning, that of the 'cosmic function' of flight – and of this the bird itself was a living hieroglyph. The symbol evoked this 'cosmic function' and one who read it properly could participate in it, could feel the forces behind existence at work, what the Egyptians called the *neters*. With *symbolique* one looked not only at the world, but into it.

This ability to look into the world, to see it from the inside, is a central theme in the knowledge of the imagination. It recurs repeatedly throughout its history, appearing in many forms. In the next chapter we will look at how one individual, a poet and scientist, managed to regain a sense of our lost participation, and how from this he developed an entire philosophy of nature.

Chapter Three
The Knower and the Known

In the wee hours of 3 September 1786, Johann Wolfgang von Goethe – the great German poet, whose early work, *The Sorrows of Young Werther* (1774), was said to have taught Europe how to cry – slipped out of Carlsbad, where he had recently celebrated his thirty-seventh birthday, and began his trek to 'the land where the citron blooms', Italy, in the uncomfortable confines of a mail coach. His friends in Weimar, where he had been living at the court of the young Grand Duke Karl August – who had made Goethe a Privy Councillor some years earlier – were surprised at his sudden departure, but Goethe brushed aside all concern about this. Goethe could be an exemplar of urbanity and decorum, but if needs demanded, he could also be rude. Weimar had become stifling. He had learned much and developed significantly during his time there – and development was something that preoccupied Goethe profoundly – but he felt stalled, hemmed in by his obligations and responsibilities. So, requesting a sudden leave of absence from the Duke, and speaking vaguely of a mineralogical excursion into the nearby mountains, Goethe, with minimum baggage, no servant, and an assumed name – Möller – headed south. He was gone for two years.

His account of his travels, Goethe's *Italian Journey,* not published until 1816, is a remarkable work, but it is not entirely one that a poet would be expected to produce. It contains much of what the standard travel book should. Goethe relates encounters with the people he meets, talks about the unusual customs he is discovering, describes his experience viewing the ruins of classical civilisation and the great art that spans the centuries. He had some interesting encounters indeed: in Sicily he met the family of the great Freemason or charlatan – depending on your perspective – Cagliostro, and while he was in Naples Vesuvius seemed to acknowledge his presence with an eruption. But readers coming to the work without some prior knowledge of Goethe's interests may be surprised at the *scientific* tone of much of the book. Goethe's *Italian Journey* is as much an account of scientific fieldwork as it is an account of a poet's travels in a strange land, perhaps even more so.

Surprising as this may sound, in Goethe's case it really should not be, because Goethe considered himself a poet *and* a scientist. Indeed not long before his death in 1832, Goethe told his friend Johann Peter Eckermann that he believed his scientific work was more important than his poetry, an opinion not necessarily shared by many others, scientists and poets included.[1] If Owen Barfield was a hedgehog, holding tight to his one big thing, Goethe was most definitely a fox – one with a keen interest in many different things, one of which was science, or the 'natural philosophy' out of which what we know as science emerged.

Goethe's *Italian Journey* is filled with precise descriptions of the topography, geology, minerals, meteorological conditions, animal behaviour and other objective 'facts' about the land he is travelling through. Consider a passage describing his entry to Bavaria. Stopping at the monastery of Waldsassen, Goethe notes the 'saucer or basin-like hollow' in which the monastery stands; the soil, which is a 'decomposed clayey slate', made 'loose and fertile' because of the quartz from the surrounding rock formations; and the gradual rise of the terrain and the movement of its streams towards 'the Eger and the Elbe'. He remarks that he can always get a 'topographical idea of a region' by noting the direction of its streams, and then goes on to comment about the 'first class high road of granite sand' on which his coach finds itself rumbling.[2]

This is the kind of meticulous factual recording that we might expect from a geographer or mineralogist, but not necessarily from the poet who once spoke of the 'inmost, sacred warmth of the life of Nature' and of the 'overwhelming abundance' he felt as the 'glorious forms of infinite Creation moved' in his soul.[3] In both cases – *Werther* and Italy – Goethe is writing about Nature, but the nature that appears in each seems radically different. The Goethe who eagerly notes down the gradual movement of a stream to its drainage basin and the one who warbles on about the effect of nature on his soul seem two different people. Yet the nature being written about and the person doing the writing are in each instance the same.

When Goethe's artist friends in Rome – the last leg of his journey – saw the book years after his visit, they were appalled. He practically ignored many of the most well-known masterpieces, and his accounts of the ones he did see led his friends to say that 'he must have gone through Italy blindfolded', his remarks about these works being either banal or seemingly wrongheaded.[4] Goethe certainly hadn't travelled through the land of the citrons with his eyes closed and in fact one of the things Goethe went to Italy to do was to improve his drawing, and his study of the great works he did see helped him there. But although Goethe was, of course, a lover of classical art, a stronger passion grabbed him on his journey.

As he found himself moving from Carlsbad to Verona, Venice, Naples and Rome, he saw that he was more and more absorbed in his observations about the countryside, its flora and fauna. His perception of nature had cooled somewhat from how he depicted it in the passion-soaked pages of *Werther*. He was of course no longer the twenty-five year old whose novel about unrequited love ending in suicide triggered a rash of copycat self-deaths across the continent. But something more than the natural cooling of ardour that happens with age was at work. Although *Werther* had got the *Sturm und Drang* ball rolling, and it was now barrelling away as Romanticism swept across Europe, Goethe had for some time turned his back on the overwrought emotionality and morbid sensitivity that afflicted his tragic hero and his many epigones. He wanted to see nature as it was in itself, and not as a convenient pegboard for our conflicting emotions, a practice in which the Romanticism that he spawned had, he believed, overindulged.

Goethe turned to natural philosophy as a corrective to the debilitating subjectivity that he felt was encouraged by a too acute attentiveness to one's feelings. This movement from intense subjectivity to a rigorously imposed objective discipline is not uncommon among German speaking poets. In the early twentieth century, the Austrian poet Rainer Maria Rilke followed Goethe in this, although his needed rigour came from the advice of the sculptor Rodin, for whom he worked as a secretary for a time in

Paris, rather than science. Rodin advised the young poet to forget his feelings and take a good look at *things,* to, in a sense, sculpt his poems in the way that he, Rodin, did his statues.[5] The result was a breakthrough in Rilke's work, the *Ding Gedichte* or 'thing poems' recorded in his *New Poems.* These works try to capture the hard reality of their subject, and not merely express the poet's feelings about them.

Half a century earlier than Rilke, a young Friedrich Nietzsche – as much a poet-philosopher as Goethe was a scientist-poet – cooled his heated Romantic brow by taking up the discipline of philology – the study of ancient languages – and abandoning his idea of becoming a composer.[6] His oversensitive system needed something repetitious and methodical to keep it from going to extremes. Each of these poets in their own way realised that too much indulgence in emotion, too many ecstasies and excitements, would prove harmful to them.

Of the three, Goethe was perhaps the strongest – at least he lived longer than the other two. But his turn to the objective world was not motivated by a complete rejection of poetry, nor did it result in the kind of science based on the new way of knowing that appeared in the early seventeenth century. What Goethe wanted to achieve was a kind of 'poetic science', a natural philosophy based not on seeing the world as a kind of machine, but one based on seeing it, participating with it imaginatively, as a living intelligence. We can say that if Goethe wanted to bring some objectivity to his perception of nature, he also wanted to bring some subjectivity to it, but a different kind than he had before. We can say that it was a kind of 'objective subjectivity'. As Barfield was interested in doing, he wanted to see the inside of the world.

Goethe's desire to grasp Nature's secrets – or God's; the two were often synonymous for him – started early on. At the age of nine he built an altar to Nature out of material from his father's natural history collection; this he decorated with candles, which he lit as a sign of his devotion and the solemnity of the occasion. Even then he had a vague feeling that he would, at some point, develop a kind of 'mystical religion' of his own.[7] Such thoughts should not strike us as strange, coming from a boy his age, as the part of Germany where Goethe was born – Frankfurt-am-Main – was associated with the Pietist religious movement of the previous century. Pietism placed great emphasis on personal experience and depth of spirituality, rather than religious dogma, and as Ronald Gray in *Goethe the Alchemist* argues, the Pietism of Goethe's time was often associated with the more serious side of alchemy.[8] Alchemy is concerned with the transformation of matter, with its metamorphosis from a lowly state – lead – into a more noble one – gold – although whether it is concerned with an inner transformation of the alchemist, rather than an outer transformation of physical matter, remains debatable. But if there was one central idea informing the 'mystical religion' Goethe would spend his life articulating in different ways, we can say that it too concerned itself with this kind of metamorphosis: how the mysterious and universal force of life transformed itself into its endless variety of forms.

Goethe's literary talent showed itself early on too; even before he had erected his altar to Nature, he had written a play. By his early teens he was studying Plato, Aristotle, and the mystical Plotinus. His first plan was to study law, which he did for two years in Leipzig. But on his return to Frankfurt his interest in uncovering the secrets of nature took a more inward turn. He became involved with a group of Pietists, of whom the religious writer Suzanne von Klettenberg was the most prominent, and through her he began a serious study of alchemical, Hermetic, and spiritual literature, absorbing difficult texts by Paracelsus, Basil Valentine, J.B. van Helmont and George Starkey.

Von Klettenberg and her fellow Pietists were well versed in the obscure writings of the sixteenth century Bohemian theosophist Jacob Boehme, whose dark visions have influenced a number of important thinkers, among them the philosophers Hegel and Heidegger, the poets Blake and Coleridge, as well as the religious writer Martin Buber and the psychologist C.G. Jung. One morning, the 'mystic cobbler', as Boehme was called – he made his living making shoes – was transfixed by the sight of sunlight reflected off a dish. He suddenly felt as if he saw into the heart of nature and could understand the secret of everything around him. As his early biographer Abraham von Franckenberg recounted, Boehme had been 'introduced into the innermost ground or centre of the recondite or hidden nature', and he perceived what he later

called 'the signature of things', their inmost essence.[9] Boehme
was so startled by the experience that he walked into some nearby
fields in order to shake it off, but it persisted. He felt that he was
actually seeing into the trees, leaves, and grass around him. He felt
as if he learned 'more in one quarter of an hour' than he would
have had he spent years at university. Boehme tried to convey
his vision in a series of books whose deep import is recognisable,
even with their dense obscurity. He wrote in a regrettably opaque
alchemical language, borrowing much from the sixteenth century
Swiss alchemist and physician Paracelsus, who had himself earlier
claimed that 'we may look into Nature in the same way that the
sun shines through a glass'.[10]

It was this interior vision that motivated Goethe's Pietist friends,
and Goethe had an opportunity to benefit from some of its practical
application. On his return from Leipzig Goethe's health suffered
and he experienced something of a nervous breakdown. Among
those attending von Klettenberg's Pietist meetings was a certain
Dr Metz, who often alluded to a mysterious 'Universal Medicine'
of whose secrets he was aware. Dr Metz spoke of certain books
and writings through the study of which one could possess this
medicine. Goethe's mother, a member of the Pietist group, knew of
Metz's claims and, fearful of her son's health – Goethe's condition
seemed to be worsening – begged Dr Metz to use his wonder drug
on him. He did and Goethe experienced a rapid and inexplicable –
from conventional medicine's point of view – recovery.[11]

Following his miraculous cure, Goethe plunged deeper into
his alchemical studies, beginning the kind of 'hands on' scientific
work he would continue throughout his career. Goethe set up
an alchemical laboratory in his parents' attic. Here he collected a
furnace, a retort, some alembics and a sand-bath, and set to work in
order to produce *liquor silicium* or 'flint juice', a product of melting
down pure quartz with a mixture of alkali. If successful, this
operation should result in a kind of transparent glass, of remarkable
clarity, which dissolves on contact with air. Goethe wanted to
achieve the *liquor silicium* because it would serve for him as his
alchemical *prima materia,* the first, or 'primal' matter, the base
from which the alchemical work of transformation would proceed.
Goethe worked hard at capturing his 'flint juice', but to no avail,

and after several attempts he had to admit defeat. Yet the desire to arrive at a 'primal' phenomenon remained and would inspire his later scientific work.

Goethe pursued his law studies in Strasbourg, and while there he had an experience that would shape his later investigations into Nature's secrets. Like many who visited the city, Goethe was struck by its Gothic cathedral which, for more than two centuries, was the world's tallest building.[12] Its height was especially striking for Goethe who, at that time, 1770, was twenty-one years old and suffering from vertigo. The cathedral fascinated Goethe and he observed it under a number of different conditions, being especially attentive to the way in which varying angles of light affected its appearance. He said that in it 'the sublime has entered into alliance with the pleasing'.[13] He made many sketches of the cathedral, trying to observe it from as many perspectives as he could, even forcing himself to climb its tower, in order to cure himself of his vertigo. At a small, unprotected platform just below the tower's summit, Goethe would repeatedly endure the giddiness that came over him, until he had conquered it.

Just before leaving Strasbourg to return to Frankfurt, Goethe mentioned to some friends that, in his opinion, the tower was incomplete, and he made a sketch of what it would have looked like, had the original designed been followed.[14] A friend who knew of the cathedral's original plans confirmed that Goethe's suspicions were correct; indeed the tower as they knew it was not as it had initially been planned and Goethe's sketch had got it right. Goethe's friend asked him who had told him of this, as it was not common knowledge. Goethe replied that the tower itself had told him: 'I observed it so long and so attentively and I bestowed on it so much affection that it decided at the end to reveal to me its manifest secret'. As Hans Gebert, writing of Goethe's experience at Strasbourg Cathedral, remarked: 'Through observation, exercise, and mental effort he had penetrated to an imperceptible reality, the idea of the architect'.[15] That is to say that through his imagination, Goethe had hit on knowledge that was otherwise inaccessible. What helped Goethe here was his 'developed inner life', what the philosopher Robert McDermott describes as 'the painstakingly trained process by which the sympathetic personal knower imaginatively gleans the ideal form of each physical object and natural process'.[16]

Long and attentive observation of and affection toward the world around him were on Goethe's mind as his coach led him deeper into the land where the citron blooms. He had by this time established himself as, if not a professional, then at least a highly talented amateur naturalist, having in 1784 shown that the human anatomy contained the intermaxillary bone. Prior to this the perceived absence of this small bone in human anatomy was taken as evidence that human beings were something apart from the rest of creation; they had a special dispensation from God and were set apart from other animals, that possessed the bone. Goethe discovered the presence of the intermaxillary bone in humans by observing and comparing human and animal skulls. The bone is located in the jaw and as Goethe looked and reflected on the similarities in shape among the different skulls before him, there it was. 'Eureka', he wrote to his friend the philosopher Johann Herder, who, like Owen Barfield, was deeply interested in the evolution of language. 'I have found neither gold nor silver, but something that unspeakably delights me,' he told Herder. It was the intermaxillary bone.

Darwin was later to credit Goethe's discovery as the starting point of our real understanding of evolution. Goethe was not around to accept Darwin's compliment; he died some years before *The Origin of Species* was published in 1859. I suspect he would have acknowledged it gracefully but I also believe he would have with equal grace pointed out to Darwin and to his followers, that his own ideas about evolution were rather different from theirs. He did not see it as a mechanical process, driven by 'natural selection,' 'survival of the fittest' and accidental mutations brought about by sheer chance. On the contrary, evolution for Goethe was the sign of an intelligent force working from *within* outward, rather than the result of purely external factors impinging on a passive, reactive matter. Nature was a great alchemist and in its manifold forms Goethe saw the active, creative response of life to the surroundings in which it found itself, as well as the growth and development of its own inherent purposiveness, its own self-direction. For Goethe life was not some infinitely plastic stuff that would passively submit to the push and pull of the environment, but an intelligent creative force that took advantage of the conditions in which it found itself in order to actualise to the optimum its inherent possibilities.

It was for evidence of this mysterious, hidden, but ever present force that Goethe sought as his coach drew him into the sunshine of the south. By this time his interest in the forms that life takes had shifted from the animal world to that of the plants. He was in pursuit of what he called the *Urpflanze* or 'primal plant'. In a letter to Herder he described it as 'the strangest creature in the world, which Nature herself shall envy me'. It was the key to 'the secret of the reproduction and organisation of plants', yet at the same time was 'the simplest thing imaginable'. With it, Goethe was confident that 'it will be possible to go on for ever inventing plants and know that their existence is logical'. What this meant is that if such plants do not already exist, 'they could, for they are not the shadowy phantoms of vain imagination, but possess an inner necessity and truth'.[17]

What Goethe meant by this 'inner necessity and truth' is what his younger contemporary, the poet Samuel Taylor Coleridge, spoke of as 'facts of mind'. For both Goethe and Coleridge, the imagination was not merely a loosening of reason and a setting free of uncontrolled fantasy – as the Enlightenment regarded it – but a cognitive power that obeyed its own rules and disciplines. These were other than those associated with the analytical reasoning that informed most of the burgeoning science of Goethe's and Coleridge's time – and which has dominated it up until today. But they were nevertheless in their own way just as demanding and rigorous. But what was essential in what we can call 'the imaginative method' was the *way* in which phenomena, whether a plant or a work of architecture, were observed.

That the poetic and the scientific – imagination and knowledge – were never far apart in Goethe's mind is clear from his account of how he first saw the 'primal plant'. Goethe was not subject to the dichotomy of 'two cultures', the bifurcation of science and the humanities at the heart of C.P. Snow's once influential book. (And that science should itself be something apart from the study of what makes us human gives pause for thought.) On 17 January 1787, Goethe was on his way to the Public Gardens in Palermo,

Sicily, 'with the firm intention of meditating further upon my poetic dreams', when there was a sudden change in plans. The poem he was working on, inspired by the clear Mediterranean sky, could wait – 'Nausicaa' remained a fragment – but something equally if not more poetic seized his attention. He reflected that here, where 'instead of being grown in pots or under glass' as they were back in Weimar, plants were 'allowed to grow freely in the open and fresh air and fulfil their destiny', they became more intelligible. Faced with the variety of such specimens before him, 'an old fancy' suddenly captured his mind. 'Among this multitude,' Goethe thought, 'might I not discover the Primal Plant?' That there must be such a thing Goethe was forced to accept, 'otherwise how could I recognise that this or that form *was* a plant if all were not built upon the same basic model?'[18]

What was – or is – Goethe's Primal Plant? Many have tried to explain it and Goethe himself was aware of the difficulty in doing so. 'My theory is difficult to describe,' he confided in a journal. 'No matter how clearly and exactly it is written down, it is impossible to understand merely from reading'.[19] Goethe's remark tells us that what is important in being able to understand his idea is that one should have the kind of experience that enabled Goethe to see his Primal Plant. One could know it adequately only in this way, and this required a special effort of imagination, what Goethe called 'active seeing', something different from the passive reflection we usually consider 'seeing' to be. Goethe's 'active seeing' is similar to the effort that Owen Barfield suggested was needed in order to experience 'participation' consciously. In essence Goethe and Barfield are speaking of the same thing: using the imagination as a means of knowledge.

Goethe's *Urpflanze* was – or is – a kind of botanical Platonic Form, an ideal model from which all actual plants emerge. In Jungian terms we can say it is the 'archetypal' plant. Yet it differs from Plato's forms and Jung's archetypes in that, at least according to Goethe, the *Urpflanze* can actually be seen. Plato's Forms are not sensible. They cannot be seen directly, but we can see the physical phenomena in which they manifest, and we can grasp their reality intellectually, that is, through the mind. Likewise, Jung maintained that we can never experience the archetypes directly, because it is through them that we have experience, rather as the philosopher Kant maintained that we know the world through what he called categories that we do not perceive but through which we have perceptions.

Goethe's *Urpflanze* – or *Urphänomena,* as there are more than one 'primal phenomena' – is something different. Jumping ahead a bit we can say that it occupies a kind of middle ground between physical, sensible things, and pure concepts, between the phenomena of the senses and the ideas of the intellect. We can say they exist in what the philosopher and religious scholar Henry Corbin called 'the Imaginal', the realm of images, that has its home in our interior world.

Goethe's insistence that he could actually see the *Urpflanze* later got him into an argument with his friend, the poet Friedrich Schiller. Schiller, too, was interested in science. Goethe was initially not partial to his younger contemporary, finding his literary work – in particular his play, *The Robbers* – too much informed by the overheated Romanticism from which he had weaned himself. But a correspondence had developed between them and in the spring of 1794 the two met at a scientific conference in Jena. Goethe had by this time published his botanical work *The Metamorphosis of Plants* (1790) in which he presented his theory of the *Urpflanze* and his method of perceiving it. Although Goethe was famous throughout Europe, the work was so radical that his usual publisher had rejected it, and he had to use another.[20]

After a lecture Goethe and Schiller fell into conversation. Schiller said something that struck Goethe as insightful. Schiller remarked that the 'dissecting manner' in which the lecturer had spoken of the scientific study of nature, could not appeal to the layman – pre-echoing here William Wordsworth's oft-quoted line that 'we murder to dissect'.[21] Goethe agreed but went on to say that such a manner, in which Nature was cut up into ever smaller bits and pieces – the work of the left brain – should not appeal to the professionals either. He told Schiller that 'perhaps there was still the possibility of another method, one which would not tackle Nature by merely dissecting and particularising, but show her at work and alive, *manifesting herself in her wholeness in every single part of her being'.*[22]

Schiller agreed and was intrigued by Goethe's remarks and expressed an interest in hearing more. The walk from the lecture hall to Schiller's house – he lived in Jena – was, according to Erich Heller, 'the dramatic climax in the history of German thought and letters'. Anyone overhearing them along the way would have eavesdropped on what was ostensibly 'merely a discussion about the growth of vegetables'. But as Heller makes clear, what they were really discussing was 'the human mind and its search for truth'.[23]

When they arrived at Schiller's home Goethe went into more detail. He explained 'with great vivacity' his book on plant metamorphosis. He then drew a quick sketch of the Primal Plant, which Schiller regarded with 'great interest and intelligence'. Yet after considering all Goethe had said, in the end Schiller shook his head. 'This,' Schiller said, 'had nothing to do with *experience*'. It was only 'an idea'.

This angered Goethe because it reminded him of a basic difference between himself and Schiller. Schiller accepted the philosopher Kant's firm distinction between experience and ideas, between what we can have direct, sensory knowledge of and what we can only think about. For him, Goethe's Primal Plant was not something he could see, but only something he could think about. It was only an idea, like others, and no more 'real' than they. Goethe, ever tactful, repressed his anger and turned Schiller's reservations back on him. 'Well,' Goethe said, 'so much the better. It means that I have ideas without knowing it, and can even *see them with my eyes*'.[24]

'Seeing ideas with one's eyes' could be a way of describing what Goethe went about when he perceived the Primal Plant. Goethe's approach to observation was rather different from what had become the accepted method since the early seventeenth century. Where the new way of knowing demanded that the observer remain detached, isolated from the observed, so as to capture it in complete 'objectivity', thereby making what was under observation an 'object' – denying it had any 'inside' – Goethe knew that such objectivity was impossible. Well before Werner Heisenberg, Goethe had grasped this central truth, that 'the phenomenon is not detached from the observer, but intertwined and involved with him'.[25] Heisenberg's 'uncertainty principle' is credited with the recognition that the observer through his observation alters the observed; in the case of elementary particles, this makes it impossible for us to know the position and speed of a particle simultaneously; we can only know one or the other, hence, the 'uncertainty'. Yet in 1932 Heisenberg recognised Goethe's primacy here and lamented that the trajectory of science since Goethe's day had renounced 'the aim of bringing the phenomena of nature to our thinking in an immediate and living way', and led to a practice less and less concerned with an 'understanding of the world'.[26]

What Heisenberg meant was that science's plunge into the dimension behind or beneath phenomena – into the bizarre world of elementary particles, smaller and smaller bits and pieces – separated it more and more from any kind of human world, the world of clouds, trees, mountains and forests. But it was precisely the participation of the human and Nature, mind and matter, that Goethe believed was the true subject of science.

Where the new way of knowing required that the observer remain passive, so as not to taint what he was observing with his 'subjectivity' – Thomas Huxley, Darwin's 'bulldog', advises us to 'sit down before fact like a little child' – Goethe, as we've seen, took a more active approach.[27] Like Schwaller de Lubicz's 'intelligence of the heart', Goethe wants to get *inside* phenomena, not behind them to some 'really real' world, whether of elementary particles or Kant's *ding-an-sich,* the 'thing-in-itself' forever barred from our cognition by the 'categories' of thought. The truth of the world, Goethe maintains, is given immediately. Nature, for Goethe, is not hidden, or if she is, it is in plain sight. Naked is the best disguise. Her secrets are manifest, if we know how to look for them.[28] 'Nature,' Goethe wrote, 'has nether kernel nor shell; she is everything at once'. As Heller writes: 'what is within and what is without are for Goethe merely poles of one and the same thing'.

If this is so, then what is going on inside the observer is at least as important as what is going on outside him, what, that is, he is observing. Our attitude toward what we are observing will determine what we see. If we are determined that what lies before us is merely a piece of complicated machinery, as many who engaged in the new way of knowing did, then that is what we will see. If we believe that the only way to understand the world is to break it down into smaller and smaller parts, then smaller and smaller bits and pieces are what we shall find.

Yet we've seen that Goethe had a different aim in mind. He wanted to see Nature 'manifesting herself in her wholeness in every single part of her being'. Earlier I referred to Ernst Jünger's idea of 'stereoscopy', a way of looking at things that presents their surface and depth simultaneously. Jünger was a modern-day Goethean scientist, at least his attitude toward Nature was very much along Goethean lines; readers of his anti-Nazi parable *On The Marble Cliffs* know this. Like Goethe, he aimed to see inside and outside simultaneously. This requires an effort of imagination, a gesture of getting in rapport with what you are observing.

Goethe observed phenomena not with the cold detachment of the mechanical scientist, but with the warmth and involvement of the artist, even, perhaps, the lover. This was not the same as the kind of emotional projection that Goethe wrote out of his system in *Werther*. That kind of subjectivity did need to be inhibited. Goethe did not project his emotions on to the natural world, as if he was spraying paint onto a blank wall. Goethe's 'lover' here was somewhat more mature. What he did do was to direct an inner warmth and attentiveness to what he was observing; he became involved in it in the same way that an artist becomes involved in the subject of his work.[29] Goethe observed his plant in all stages of development, from seed to flower, patiently following it in its process of growth. He would then imagine the plant, building up an inner vision of it, recreating it in his mind, and following this too through its development. Nature gave herself all at once, but she was never static, fixed, immobile, but was always in transformation, metamorphosis, growing from the simple to the complex. We can say that where the quantitative approach to Nature took very precise snapshots of her at selected moments, freezing her constant flow into a fixed form so that it could be 'pinned down', Goethe's way was to slow his own consciousness down, so that he could see the growth of a plant as a whole.

Yet at each moment of development, the whole is wholly given and for one engaged in Goethe's active seeing, it is visible. 'To recognise living forms *as such*, to see in context their visible and tangible parts, to perceive them as manifestations of *something within,* and thus to master them, to a certain extent, in *wholeness* through a concrete vision', what Goethe called *Anschauung,* a 'direct perception': such was the aim of Goethe's morphological investigations.[30]

Goethe's attentiveness to phenomena was acute. The poet W.H. Auden, one of the translators of the *Italian Journey,* said that Goethe 'makes enormous efforts ... to say exactly what shape and colour an object is, and precisely where it stands in spatial relation to other objects ...' At times such attention to detail gives the *Italian Journey* a somewhat stilted feel, Goethe's meticulous observation stopping the narrative flow; Auden even makes an oblique comparison with the static *nouveau roman* of the French novelist Alain Robbe-Grillet, known for his obsessive, paralysing descriptions. But this attention is at the heart of Goethean science, as it is at the heart of a method of philosophy that would emerge in the century after Goethe's death. I'm referring to the 'phenomenology' developed by Edmund Husserl, mentioned earlier in this book.

Husserl was appalled at the state philosophy had gotten into by the early twentieth century and believed it was time for a new beginning. His philosophical battle cry was 'To the things themselves!' This meant that philosophy had to return from the abstract realms it had lost itself in with Hegel and the relativistic view it had adopted through what was known at the time as 'psychologism', the belief that philosophical problems originate in the human psyche, and had no 'reality' of their own; this is not radically different from how much of contemporary neuroscience sees them today. Husserl called for a new, rigorous and thorough approach involving an acute observation and description of *phenomena.* Hence his method was known as 'phenomenology', an attempt to arrive at a detailed, accurate account of things as they appear to us, as they are 'given' in our consciousness, forgetting questions about their reality or essence.

Hegel had, of course, earlier used the term phenomenology in *The Phenomenology of Mind,* his account of the different forms mind or spirit takes in its manifestation in human history (the German word *Geist,* which Hegel uses, can be translated into English as either 'mind' or 'spirit'). Husserl was not interested in a historical account of consciousness, as Barfield was, although in other ways their insights support each other. His focus was on consciousness as we experience it now, as given. His central insight was that our perception of things is *intentional.* In its simplest form this means that consciousness is always consciousness *of* something. It is directed at a target. There is always a subject, the mind that is conscious, and an object, what it is consciousness of. The object of consciousness can be a tree, the idea of a tree, an image of one, or a memory of one: in all cases, consciousness's relation to it is nonetheless 'intentional'.

This seems evident enough and Husserl's ideas spawned much of early twentieth century 'continental' philosophy, giving birth not only to phenomenology, but through his one-time student and friend Martin Heidegger, existentialism. Later phenomenologists took Husserl's cues and developed them in ways that differed profoundly from the master; Heidegger himself was the most famous example here, transforming Husserl's focus on consciousness to what Heidegger called the 'question of being', and moving from phenomenology to 'fundamental ontology'. Max Scheler, who I write about in *The Caretakers of the Cosmos,* developed an approach that differed from both Husserl and Heidegger. Where Husserl wanted to save philosophy from relativism by developing a rigorous method that would make it a kind of science, Scheler saw phenomenology as more of an attitude, a *Geisteshaltung,* or 'disposition of spirit', that he likened to love, a 'phenomenological love' along the lines of Goethe's 'attentiveness'.[31]

Husserl's writings are dense and opaque and his ideas are expressed in a typically difficult abstract prose. But the basic vision that emerges from them is that Husserl believed consciousness was not only intentional, that is directed at a target, but was also in some strange way involved in the *coming into being* of whatever it was directed at. That is to say that consciousness was creative, or, at the least, 'participatory' in the way that both Barfield and Goethe believed.

The basic 'act' of phenomenology is what Husserl calls 'stepping out of the natural standpoint'. I mentioned the 'natural standpoint' in the last chapter. It is basically our immediate unquestioned acceptance of the world as 'given', as 'there', whether we are or not, and ourselves as passive observers of this fact. Husserl said that the natural stance of the waking ego is a perceiving, a 'looking'. But when we step out of the natural standpoint and perform what Husserl calls the *epoché,* a temporary suspension of belief in everything we think we know about the world, the relation of consciousness to the world changes. The world no longer seems to be something simply 'there' that our consciousness somehow mirrors. Our perceiving seems somehow more 'active'. We become aware of the dynamic character of our perception, something that is obscured when we are within the natural standpoint – in other words, most of the time.[32]

It may seem that stepping out of the natural standpoint is an easy affair. It is not. It takes much effort and is difficult to sustain. It does not consist of merely saying to yourself 'Okay. For the next ten minutes I will not believe in everything I do believe about the world', and then agreeing to a number of absurd proposals. During those ten minutes you may agree that the moon may be made of Swiss cheese, but you really know it isn't, no matter what you say. Your token agreement did not in any way upset your fundamental assumptions, your 'metaphysics' about the world. To truly step out of the natural standpoint means really digging down deep into yourself and making a peculiar effort of imagination and truly seeing the world free of all your assumptions about it. This is as difficult to do as any meditation and requires practice and perseverance to achieve. The sign that your efforts are bearing fruit is that what you perceive should begin to have an air of 'strangeness' about it. This should lead to a feeling of strangeness about yourself, your consciousness, an odd unfamiliarity with it, which at the same time seems familiar, as if you were remembering something you had forgotten or, in a tried and true philosophical analogy, were waking from a dream.

All philosophy requires a kind of violence, an effort to go against the current of everyday life and secure some footing from which we can contemplate it, rather than be driven headlong in its constant flow. As Whitehead said, 'It takes an extraordinary intelligence to contemplate the obvious'. But it is precisely the obvious that can lead to the most mysterious things of all.

This active character of our perception was lost on many of the phenomenologists that followed Husserl; Jean-Paul Sartre, for example, argued against it vigorously.[33] Yet the philosopher Paul Ricoeur captured it in his analysis of Husserl's philosophy. Concerning 'intentionality', Ricoeur wrote:

> By means of this reduction [the *epoché*] consciousness rids itself of a naiveté which it has beforehand, and which Husserl calls the natural attitude. This attitude consists in spontaneously believing that the world which is there is simply given. In correcting itself about this naiveté, consciousness discovers that it is in itself giving, sense-giving. The reduction does not exclude the presence of the world; it takes nothing back. It does not even suspend the primacy of intuition in every cognition. After the reduction, consciousness continues seeing, but without being absorbed in this seeing, without being lost in it. Rather, the very seeing itself is discovered as a doing (*opération*), as a producing (*oeuvre*) – once Husserl even says 'as a creating'. Husserl would be understood – and the one who thus understands him would be a phenomenologist – if the intentionality which culminates in seeing were recognised to be a creative vision.[34]

Recognising that the 'intentionality which culminates in seeing' is a 'creative vision' seems very close to how Goethe perceived the way in which we observe the world. One should also point out that Ricoeur's remark that 'after the reduction, consciousness continues seeing, but without being absorbed in this seeing, without being lost in it' has some connotations beyond Husserl's phenomenology. Being absorbed and lost in seeing, in the world, that is, seen from the natural standpoint, sounds rather like the condition of 'nescience' or 'ignorance' in Buddhism or being stuck in Maya in Hinduism or what Gurdjieff calls 'sleep': that is, a dream that is doubly deceptive because it presents itself as wakefulness. This suggests to me that although couched in very different language and motivated by what seem very different concerns, phenomenology's terrain, at least as Ricoeur seems to be presenting it, shares much with more ostensibly spiritual, esoteric or religious disciplines.[35]

Goethe's search for the *Urpflanze* may have annoyed Schiller and embarrassed botanists who felt he should have stuck to poetry. But his feud with Newton over the phenomenon of colour was even more scandalous. Like his younger contemporary William Blake, who railed against 'single vision and Newton's sleep' – championing in his own way the kind of 'double vision' we have been exploring here – in Newton, Goethe saw the emblem of the mechanical, dissecting science that he and Schiller both abhorred.[36] But where Blake devised a dramatic cosmic mythology which he expressed in epic and often obscure poems in order to submit his complaints, Goethe decided to beat Newton at his own game, and devise his own theory of colour, to show how Newton's *Opticks* (1704) had got it wrong.

Goethe believed that Newton's demonstration of how light is made up of the colours of the spectrum was arrived at by inadmissible means, rather like the confession of a prisoner obtained through torture. Newton arrived at his conclusion, Goethe argued, by subjecting light to the kind of dissection and analysis he and Schiller had agreed was an impediment to a true understanding of nature. Much has been written showing that Goethe misunderstood Newton, that his own ideas were simply absurd, or that he had no business doing science anyway, a sad example of a great mind in one field showing its utter ignorance – and egotism – in another. Goethe wanted to show that colour was not merely the effect of our subjective interpretation of a particular 'wavelengths' of light – between 400 and 700 nanometres – which sunlight can be 'broken up' into. Rather it was the result of the *polarity* between light and dark, and the 'struggle' between them. For Goethe, the colours of the spectrum are the result of the 'deeds' and 'suffering' of light.

As the reader might expect, no one, certainly not scientists, took Goethe's arguments against Newton or those supporting his own theory very seriously.[37] But the point is not so much whether Newton was right and Goethe wrong as that their approach to the phenomenon of colour was radically different. Goethe did not want to 'explain' colour, and certainly not in terms of the quantitative way of knowing that was becoming increasingly more dominant in his time. Goethe was interested in the 'phenomenology of colour', how we experience it, how colour *is* in our human world. The details of Goethe's theory can be found in his book, *Theory of Colours* (1810), and there are excellent expositions of it and instructions in how readers can make some of Goethe's observations themselves.[38] What is important here is his basic approach, which, as we've seen, involves an awareness of the involvement of the observer with the observed. Abstract colour produced mechanically under artificial conditions is not the same as colour experienced in the world, the totality of which it is a part, Goethe believed. Newton saw the spectrum in an artificially darkened room and by forcing light to pass through a series of obstacles. Goethe's observations of colour took place in normal conditions and were phenomenological in that they were focused on the 'thing itself', as it is given to is in our immediate experience.

What is in question here, as Erich Heller recognised, is not who is 'right' about colour, Newton or Goethe, but two different conceptions of knowledge. For the new way of knowing, knowledge was something 'out there', in the external world, or at least the 'facts' that make up our knowledge are. As *The X-Files* tell us, the truth is 'out there'. Goethe saw things differently. Truth for him was not wholly 'out there', as it was for the new breed of scientists, nor was it wholly 'in here', as idealist thinkers who saw everything as 'in the mind' believed. Truth was the polarity between the two, a creative tension between the subject and the object. 'Truth' for Goethe, was 'a revelation emerging at the point where the inner world of man meets external reality. It is a synthesis of world and mind'. This is so because 'there resides in the objective world an unknown law which corresponds to the unknown law within subjective experience'.[39]

Truth, then, is not something we arrive at by sitting down before facts like a child and patiently gathering them until, through sheer number, they miraculously turn into knowledge. For us to arrive at truth requires that we actively and imaginatively engage with whatever it is we are observing. That, in a sense, we meet it halfway. In Strasbourg Goethe showed that a truth not visible or measurable in any way was nevertheless discovered through his observation and imagination. Had he observed the cathedral without his 'active seeing,' trying his best to be 'objective' in the conventional sense, he would never have caught a glimpse of its 'manifest secret'. Truth requires a meeting between inner and outer in order to come into being. It was with this idea in mind that Rudolf Steiner would later take Goethe's insight and with it build a philosophy based on the necessity for the human 'inside' to complete the world 'outside'. As Steiner wrote in his early work *Goethe's Conception of the World* (1897): 'Man is not only there in order to form for himself a picture of the finished world' – which is what we assume from the natural standpoint and which forms the basis of conventional science – 'Nay, he himself cooperates in bringing the world into existence'.[40] Or, as Steiner put it somewhat differently elsewhere: 'When one who has a rich mental life sees a thousand things which are nothing to the mentally poor, this shows as clearly as sunlight that the content of reality is only the reflection of the content of our minds, and that we receive from without only the empty form'.[41]

This, of course, is a complete rejection of the 'blank slate' school of human psychology, which maintains that there is nothing in our heads until our senses put it there. Steiner via Goethe is saying the exact opposite: there is no 'outer world' until we complete it with our inner one. (And we remember that Barfield says something similar in his account of the rise of 'language' and 'the world'.) It was Goethe's 'developed inner life' that enabled him to see the manifest secret of Strasbourg Cathedral. It was also this that allowed him to catch a glimpse of the *Urpflanze* and to recognise the birth of colour through the polarities of light and dark. Goethe adapts a line from the Neoplatonic philosopher Plotinus and turns it into verse to make his point. In the *Enneads* Plotinus had written: 'To any vision must be brought an eye adapted to what is to be seen, and having some likeness to it. Never did an eye see the sun unless it had first become sun-like'. Goethe paraphrased this as: 'If the eye were not sun-like, how could we ever see light? And if God's own power did not dwell within us, how could we delight in things divine'.[42] William Blake hit the same note when, for the frontispiece of his poem 'The Gates of Paradise', he writes: 'The Sun's Light/When he unfolds it ... Depends on the Organ that beholds it'. Or in a more aggressive mood, as he often is in *The Marriage of Heaven and Hell:* 'A fool sees not the same tree as a wise man sees'. As Paracelsus and other alchemists knew, only like can know like. What we see in the outer world depends on what we bring to it. What is observed depends on the observer.

We should point out that Goethe did not want to substitute his science for Newton's. He was aware of the immense practical value of the new, quantitative science. His science would complement that, but it would also set boundaries for what it was worthwhile for us to know. What concerned Goethe was whether this practical, or, as we would say today, technological value would overshadow larger existential issues. Goethe's most famous work, *Faust,* can be seen as a study in the difference between what man can know and what he ought to know. The new way of knowing was all about knowing what we can, regardless of the consequences. For it, knowledge in itself, was good. We can understand this; after centuries of repression enforced by the Church, the intellect demanded absolute freedom. Yet although such a catholic approach to knowledge has resulted in a great many practical uses – from the keyboard I am tapping away at to the electric lights on in my study – in one sense we can say that Goethe had an even more practical sense of the value of knowledge. For him, what counted as true knowledge was what was good for man to know – something it requires wisdom, and not merely information, to grasp.

What was good for us to know, according to Goethe, was everything that helped us to understand our place in the whole, in the totality of things. What did not aid us in grasping this was secondary and of minimal use. There were limits, not to the knowable, as Kant argued, but to the kind of knowledge that would do us good; limits, that is, to the value of knowledge. Not only in practical, utilitarian ways, but in terms of our being. 'Everything that liberates our mind without at the same time imparting self-control is pernicious'.[43] 'I hate everything that merely instructs me without augmenting or directly invigorating my activity.'[44] These remarks give us an idea of how Goethe saw the value of knowledge. The second quotation was used by Nietzsche at the beginning of his early essay *On The Use and Disadvantages of History for Life* (1874). Goethe's remarks on the value of knowledge could be collected under the title: 'The Use and Disadvantages of Knowledge for Life'.

Real, useful, true knowledge for Goethe can only be obtained by the whole human being, one in whom all our faculties work in accord, not only the insatiable analytical intellect. Knowledge devoid of imagination, feeling and the senses would only lead us to distraction and dissatisfaction and to a world in which the human seems fundamentally negligible – as our contemporary science makes clear. As Heller writes: 'The anxiety that the world, in the course of its increasing analytical disruption, may approach the point where it would become poetically useless [as it has in the 'age of prose'], and a barren place for the human affections to dwell in, informs Goethe's scientific motives …'[45]

Goethe's aim was the perennial one of arriving at a conception of the 'good life', how we can best live in order to actualise the possibilities and potentialities within us. Goethe was convinced that someone 'given up to fascinations which exercise those of his faculties which have the least bearing on what he is as a person [that is the critical and analytical ones] …is merely digging away at the gulf between him and the good life'.[46] Has measuring wavelengths of electromagnetic radiation anything to do with light and colour as we experience them? Do Higgs bosons or any other elementary particle help me understand my experience and my connection to the world around me? (This was Heisenberg's reservation.) Do superstrings or selfish genes? Goethe isn't saying that these areas of inquiry should not be explored, that they should be prohibited in the way that the Church once prohibited, or at least look very askance upon, such pursuits, or their earlier equivalents. What Goethe does say is that we need to understand these things as part of our whole being, as elements in the totality that is involved in making us human and living in a human world. How far he got with this is debatable. That these questions strike many of us as naïve suggests that Goethe's concern for the good life and our means of arriving at it has fallen by the wayside, clearing the way for an increase of the kind of knowledge which he believed could only lead man to 'fret away his days in the narrowest and most joyless limitation'.[47] A science that arrives at the conclusion that the more we understand the universe the more pointless it seems strikes me as satisfying that criterion.

Goethe's ideas about science, nature, and the human imagination may not have made an impact on the scientists around him, but they did inform an important, if little known development in European philosophy which should be mentioned here. This was the *Naturphilosophie* that arose in Germany as a product of Romanticism.

Its English translation, 'philosophy of nature', does not convey the peculiar character of the movement, which for some blended 'comparative anatomy with transcendental mysticism'.[48] Unlike the 'natural philosophy' of the Anglophone world, *Naturphilosophie* was interested in the 'inner' aspect of Nature, its soul. It took its cues from Goethe's ideas about a 'living' Nature, 'manifesting herself in her wholeness in every single part of her being'.

Several thinkers fell within the *Naturphilosophie* camp, among them G.H. Schubert, Carl Gustav Carus, Alexander von Humboldt and Franz von Baader. Schubert was a physician, Carus a physiologist and painter, von Humboldt a naturalist, explorer, and geographer, and von Baader a theologian and philosopher. We could also include in their ranks Goethe's young contemporary Friedrich von Hardenberg, better known under his pen name Novalis. Like Goethe, Novalis strove to bridge the increasing gap between the critical and imaginative aspects of human consciousness.[49] In his short life – he died at the age of twenty-eight – Novalis studied mineralogy, and was an assessor of mines; he also tackled mathematics, chemistry, geology and physics as well as philosophy, esotericism and history, in the meantime writing novels and mystical poetry such as his *Hymns to the Night*.

A later exponent of *Naturphilosophie* was the German scientist and visionary Gustav Fechner, who proposed the idea that the earth was a single organism well before James Lovelock popularised the notion of 'Gaia' in the early 1970s. Following a long illness, which included blindness, Fechner had a sudden illumination. Standing in a garden he felt that 'every flower beamed upon me with a peculiar clarity, as though into the outer light it was casting its own'.[50] Fechner took from his experience the conviction that Nature, the entire universe in fact, is alive and conscious, an idea that can be traced back to the *anima mundi* of the Neoplatonists. He called the earth an angel, an insight we will return to in the next chapter.

With Goethe *Naturphilosophie* was interested in nature's transformative powers, how it 'was steadily transformed from a simpler, less organised, earlier state to a higher, more developed, later state', much as was the aim of alchemy.[51] It was also fascinated, as Goethe was, by the different forms life adopted. Like Goethe, it saw these as variations on some basic patterns, what it called 'archetypes', much in advance of C.G. Jung. These fundamental patterns seemed evidence of divine design, motifs of an intelligence at work in nature, rather than the mindless, mechanical forces that Darwin and his followers would soon discover. For these thinkers, Nature was not an infinitely plastic stuff pushed and pulled by the blind forces of the environment; she was 'self-forming', rather in the way that 'complexity theorists' speak of a 'self-organising' nature, although for *Naturphilosophie* the idea that Nature was 'intelligent' was not an obstacle.

The most influential of the *Naturphilosophen* was Friedrich von Schelling, a friend both of Goethe and Hegel. Schelling's works, *Ideas for a Philosophy of Nature* (1797), *On The World Soul* (1798) and others had a powerful impact on the burgeoning Romantic movement, and it is accurate to say that it is within the arena of art, music and poetry that *Naturphilosophie* gained the most ground. Like Goethe, Schelling was concerned with the problem of the relation of Nature to the human mind, to consciousness. Kant and his follower Johann Gottlieb Fichte had left this in a precarious state. Kant had argued that what we see as Nature is the mind's representation of a world it can never know immediately, the world of the 'thing-in-itself'. Fichte, whose work had a profound impact on a young Rudolf Steiner, had taken this further and argued in effect that Nature, the perceived external world, was really a creation of the mind. Goethe had too deep a feeling for Nature's reality to accept this, and we've seen that he argued with Schiller about Kant's distinction between what we can see and what we can only think about.

But Goethe was no philosopher – at least he felt no attraction to abstract thought. Schelling agreed with Goethe about Nature's reality and he also agreed with him that it is in the union of the mind and Nature, self-consciousness and the world it is conscious of, that genuine truth and knowledge can be obtained. The outer world of nature and our inner one of consciousness are two sides, two expressions of the same source. Schelling saw the same activities taking place in consciousness and in the outer world. For him humankind is Nature's attempt at producing a being that could understand itself; we are, in fact, Nature becoming self-conscious.

For the historian of esotericism Antoine Faivre, *Naturphilosophie* finds in the world 'symbolic implications' and 'invisible processes' that correspond to human feelings. Faivre agrees with Novalis that 'knowledge of Nature and knowledge of oneself go hand in hand' (Novalis: 'We will come to understand the world when we understand ourselves'.).[52] This is again Goethe's insight, that only like can know like. We can understand the different forms nature adopts in its development from its simplest state to its most complex, because we discover the same forms in ourselves when we strive for self-consciousness and self-understanding. As Schelling wrote in *Ideas for a Philosophy of Nature:* 'Nature should be Mind made visible, Mind the invisible Nature'.[53]

Schelling saw two fundamental forces at work both in Nature and in human consciousness, what he called 'expansion' and 'contraction'. It was through their polarity that nature expressed herself; her various forms were the result of the clash between these two fundamental opposites. Schelling's vision presented a Nature that was much more active, a 'dramatic' Nature, full of storm, stress and struggle, rather than a mechanical one, made of cogs and wheels. Goethe saw this polarity as well, and it was through these contrasting motions, what he spoke of as 'systole' and 'diastole', the contraction and relaxation of the heart, that the *Urpflanze* transforms the leaf, its basic form, into the various parts we know: stamen, pistil, flower, fruit.

These polarities would have a powerful impact on another Romantic poet who, like Goethe, was aware of the importance of imagination in our attempt to know the world: Samuel Taylor Coleridge. We will return to him further on. In the next chapter we will look at how imagination can help us in our attempt to know, not only the outer world, but inner ones too.

Chapter Four
The Way Within

In October 1913, Dr Carl Gustav Jung, once second in command to Sigmund Freud in the psychoanalytic ranks, but now recently relieved of this position, had a disturbing experience. On the train from Zürich to Schaffhausen in northern Switzerland, a journey of little more than an hour, Jung began to look at the scenery. Soon he saw more than he had bargained for. A flood of biblical proportions seemed to sweep over Europe, coming from the North Sea and washing down to the Alps. The mountains rose to protect Jung's homeland, but in the churning waters Jung saw much debris and many bodies. Then the waves were of blood. Farmland, towns, villages: all were caught in the blood-red deluge that swept across the continent, leaving destruction in its wake.

The vision – if that is what it was – lasted for most of the journey and understandably Jung was shaken by it. For years he had treated patients at the Burghözli Asylum for just such symptoms, an invasion of their waking minds by contents of the unconscious, and now it seemed that the physician would have to heal himself. His recent break with his one-time friend and mentor, Herr Dr Freud, had, he knew, unbalanced him. It was a difficult decision, but Jung could no longer accept Freud's insistence on the sexual origin of neurosis. Jung, in fact, had never accepted it wholeheartedly anyway, but the differences between himself and Freud had become too obvious to ignore and so he was forced to go his own way. The result, as was always the case with those who chose to think differently than the master, was excommunication from the psychoanalytic circle and ostracism and calumny from those who remained within it. Jung was strong and he could bear much. But perhaps this feeling of total rejection had cracked something inside him?

The feeling that something *within* him was trying to get out stayed with Jung after his experience. His dreams became even more vivid and peculiar. He saw himself sitting on a golden chair in a Renaissance setting. A white dove landed on an emerald tablet, then transformed itself into a girl. After she had turned back into a bird, the dove told Jung that it could become a girl only when the male dove was busy with the 'twelve dead'.[1] In another dream he found himself walking through an avenue of ancient tombs; when he looked at them, their inhabitants came back to life. He also caught himself at different times throughout the day fantasising about the dead returning to life and he began to feel that it was more and more difficult to stop these fantasies from taking over his consciousness. Increasingly Jung feared that, like many of his patients, he was losing his mind.

More visions came, bringing more blood and devastation. In one dream he saw Europe caught in a sudden ice age. Jung's concern for his sanity heightened; at one point, when the pressure from within increased, Jung began to sleep with a loaded pistol near his bed, so he could blow his brains out if things became too much for him. The psychic disturbances continued for some time, but Jung received an ironic relief when, in August 1914, the First World War broke out. His visions were not, it seemed, evidence that he was cracking up. They were prophetic anticipations of the catastrophe that was erupting across Europe.[2]

Jung's relief at the fact that a world war had broken out was short-lived. That his dreams and visions seemed to prophesy the war was no guarantee that his own psyche wasn't becoming unglued. Hadn't he become convinced by his study of mental patients that their fantasies often contained precognitive and prophetic elements, mixed in with the rubbish of their emotional and intellectual breakdowns? Wasn't it in fact over such peculiarities of the psyche as these that he had to break with Freud, who dismissed such notions as errant nonsense? Jung's inner oppression continued. He was experiencing what the historian of psychiatry Henri Ellenberger called a 'creative illness', 'a deep reaching interior metamorphosis', similar to the crisis that Gustav Fechner, mentioned in the last chapter, went through.[3] It was through such crises that people like Jung, Fechner, Swedenborg, Rudolf Steiner and others 'became who they were', receiving the insights and inspirations that would inform the vision they brought back with them from the abyss. All indications suggested that Jung was on his way there now. When he arrived, the really interesting events would start happening.

Jung tried different ways to quell the turbulence inside him. At one point he found some relief playing with stones and making sand castles on the shore of Lake Zürich near his home; what boaters on the lake thought of seeing Dr Jung making mud pies is unclear. Yoga exercises he had recently learned helped too. Yet Jung's need to *understand* what was happening to him compelled him to return to the brink whenever he had managed to quieten himself down. If he was going to help people with their madness, he would have to get to know his own. He knew the danger and to anchor himself in the everyday world he would repeat a kind of mantra: he was Herr Dr Jung, with a diploma to prove it, a wife, a family and a practice. Others depended on him. This served as a kind of ballast to help keep him steady in the water.

Yet after months of fighting off the feeling that he was going mad, Jung decided to change his tactic. He would no longer fend off these attacks. If he was going mad, then so be it. When the next wave of psychic pressure came, he would not fight it off. He would just let go. And so he did.

Sitting at his desk, and once again panicking with the idea that he was losing his mind, Jung let himself 'drop'. As soon as he stopped trying to fend off the oppression, something very strange happened. Jung felt the ground give way beneath him and that he was falling. He landed on what felt like a soft mass. He found that he was at the entrance to a cave; sitting there outside it was a dwarf with leathery skin. Inside the cave Jung waded through icy waters. He found a huge glowing red crystal; beneath this he found the corpse of a blond youth, a giant black scarab, then a brilliant sun. Then a geyser of blood, like the kind he had seen in his vision on the train, shot at him. This sickened Jung and he 'woke up'. Yet a dream a few days later seemed connected to his vision. Jung found himself with a brown-skinned man – rather like his leathery dwarf – and they were on their way to kill Siegfried, the hero of Wagner's *Ring Cycle*.

Jung was compelled to know what these experiences were about.

What were they trying to tell him? He could not accept them as random, nonsensical fantasies. There clearly seemed to be some intelligence behind them. But what? Jung needed to know and in order to find out he decided to deliberately induce the fantasies. As he had 'dropped down' to some strange interior world when he had stopping fighting off the feeling that he was going mad, Jung decided to use the fantasy of entering a cave or burrow as a starting point. He received some startling results.

Letting himself 'go' once again, Jung entered a cave and then found himself in a bleak lunar landscape. There he encountered two people, a white-bearded old man and a young girl. The old man was Elijah and the girl Salome, both figures from the Bible. Jung approached them and as he did they began to speak to him. Salome was blind and the two were accompanied by a huge black snake. Other figures appeared too, such as Ka, a kind of earth spirit. But the inner figure that proved most important for Jung was one named Philemon, another figure from the Bible.[4] He became a kind of 'inner guru' for Jung, informing him about the world he had entered and giving him guidance in understanding it. In the *Red Book,* the record Jung kept of what he later called his 'descent into the unconscious', Jung depicted Philemon as a bald, white-bearded old man with bull's horns and the wings of a kingfisher. In his autobiography *Memories, Dreams, Reflections* Jung recounts many 'synchronicities' – his term for 'meaningful coincidence' – surrounding this image.[5]

Philemon told Jung much, but there was one bit of information that he passed on that was the most important of all. Philemon informed Jung that 'there are things in the psyche which I do not produce but which produce themselves and have their own life'.[6] This was not an easy thing for Jung to accept. He had had difficulty in allowing the fantasies that landed him at Philemon's feet in the first place, feeling they were a betrayal of his intellectual integrity. Now he was being asked to accept that he shared his psyche with inhabitants that had their own will and identity and which were not necessarily interested in him. To put it bluntly, there were people in his head. But that was exactly what Philemon had to teach him. In a seminar given in 1925 Jung spoke about the trouble he had assimilating what Philemon told him. It was not easy to absorb the idea that the figures Jung was encountering, like Philemon, had a life of their own, and that by entering their world, he had fallen into a strange reality that somehow existed *independently* of him, as independently as the world that existed outside his front door. If this was true, then Jung – and presumably everyone else – was sharing his mind with *others*.

'As soon as one begins to watch one's mind, one begins to observe the autonomous phenomena in which one exists as a spectator,' Jung told his audience. It took some effort on Jung's part to accept this. 'It took me a long time,' he said, 'to admit to something in myself that was not myself'. It was rather like 'writing letters to a part of myself that was not myself'.[7] Jung had to teach himself how to observe his thoughts as phenomena, in the way that Goethe had observed his plants, not as expressions of his personality, but of a life other than his. Like all of us, Jung had believed that his thoughts were his, but Philemon knew better. Jung's thoughts were no more 'his' than the animals in a forest or people in a room were, nor did they depend on him to exist, as neither the animals nor the people did. They had an objective reality of their own.

Jung in fact called the world he had entered the 'objective psyche', a term that I find more profitable and helpful than his more familiar coinage of the 'collective unconscious'. 'Collective' carries unhelpful connotations of a 'group mind' or 'mass consciousness', when what Jung means is an 'unconscious' that we all share, in the sense that we all have access to it – or it has access to us – and which is beyond the contents of our own 'personal' unconscious, which is peculiarly ours. The idea of a collective unconscious also has racial connotations and suggests a kind of psychic sediment, built up over millennia, rather like the silt that builds up at a river's delta. But Jung seems to be saying – or at least Philemon does – that there are things in 'his', or 'our' psyche, that *have nothing to do with us*. They are not the residue of countless aeons of human experience, but seem to be manifestations of some 'other' world, some strange dimension of reality that intersects with ours in an unaccountable way in our minds.

Jung was not the only one to recognise this. Some years after Jung's encounter with Philemon, Aldous Huxley wrote about his own inner travels, facilitated by the use of the drug mescaline and other means. Huxley wrote that 'Like the earth of a hundred years ago' – Huxley was writing in 1956 – 'our mind still has its darkest Africas, its unmapped Borneos and Amazonian basins'. Huxley agreed that the creatures that inhabit these 'far continents' of the mind – its 'antipodes', what Huxley called 'Mind at Large' – seem 'improbable', yet they are nonetheless 'facts of observation', which argued for their 'complete autonomy' and 'self-sufficiency'.[8] Huxley wrote these words in his little book *Heaven and Hell,* a follow up to his first foray into the mind's antipodes, *The Doors of Perception*. He got the title from an earlier inner voyager – a 'psychonaut', to use Ernst Jünger's phrase – whose work was an influence on Jung, the eighteenth century scientist and religious thinker, Emanuel Swedenborg.

Critics of Jung have argued that his celebrated 'descent into the unconscious' was nothing more than a psychotic episode. Put briefly, for them, Jung had a breakdown following his break-up with Freud, and that's the end of it. Such sentiments are not uncommon. More than a century before Jung's experience, Swedenborg faced accusations of madness and an attempt to have him put in an asylum. It failed and Swedenborg remained free, but his accounts of his journeys to heaven and hell led many to speculate that he was insane.[9] It is a longstanding truism that one man's vision is another man's madness. It's to be expected that Freudians would take the view that Jung had simply cracked up, and that this judgment would be shared by most 'rationally' minded people. We can be more generous and give Jung the benefit of the doubt and accept that his conversations with Philemon were something more than the symptoms of psychosis. We can extend this to other visionaries and accept that their visions were also 'true'. But this still leaves us with the problem of exactly how we can judge whether a vision or mystical experience is 'objective', that is real, and not only imaginary in the negative sense.

Such concerns are not limited to hard-nosed realists, eager to cut all pretentions to some 'other reality' down to size. The problem of 'false imagination' has occupied visionaries and their fellow travellers for some time. Paracelsus, the great sixteenth century alchemist, made a distinction between 'true imagination', what he called *imaginatio vera*, and mere fantasy, which he spoke of as the 'madman's cornerstone' and an 'exercise of thought without foundation in nature'.[10] Paracelsus knew the power of the imagination, which he called our 'inner firmament', the universe that extends within us in the same way that the astronomical universe extends outside us. He knew it had the power to heal, but also to kill. He famously said that: 'It is possible that my spirit … through an ardent will alone, and without a sword, can stab and wound others'. Paracelsus knew of psychosomatic illnesses well before modern science acknowledged them; in his *Opus Paramirum* (1531) – 'Work Beyond Wonders' – he speaks of 'illnesses of the imagination', in advance of both what we know of psychosomatic problems and Freudian neurosis. He seems to have anticipated the poet and magician W.B. Yeats' remark that 'whatever we build in the imagination will accomplish itself in the circumstances of our lives'.[11] A similar awareness of the concrete power of the imagination led Owen Barfield to impress upon his readers the need for a 'responsibility of the imagination', an awareness that what we think inside our heads does not necessarily stay there.[12]

We've seen that Goethe made the point of insisting to Johann Herder that, having found the 'secret of the reproduction and organisation of plants' in his *Urpflanze* and thence being able, at least in principle, to 'go on forever inventing plants', he was nevertheless assured of their 'logical' consistency. Such plants may not already exist, he said, but they could, 'for they are not the shadowy phantoms of vain imagination, but possess an inner necessity and truth'. The non-existing plants that Goethe could hypothetically create would not be monsters in the original sense of the word – aberrations of nature – but in perfect keeping with Nature's designs. This is because Goethe had matched the 'unknown law' in the outer world, Nature, with the 'unknown law' in his inner one, his imagination. As I mentioned, these 'unknown laws' are what Coleridge called 'facts of mind', *necessities* of the imagination, that must be met in order for it to be something more than a 'madman's cornerstone'. Failing this, imagination sinks to being merely what Coleridge called 'fancy', which is nothing more than 'a mode of Memory', a way of re-arranging elements obtained through the senses ('flying pigs'), which is all the 'blank slate' school of psychology will allow us. Or worse, it becomes a *distortion* of reality, Paracelsus's 'madman's cornerstone' or the kinds of images being produced by much of modern art that Barfield found indicative of a spiritual bankruptcy and which, with something like Yeats' warning in mind, he feared could eventually produce a 'fantastically hideous world'.[13]

We can see then that true inner voyagers are aware of the problem of gauging the reality of their experiences. They don't accept everything, as the simple-minded or mad would, nor do they reject it all, as tough-minded realists would. As scientists of the outer world do, they have to gather material, sort their facts, apply their critical intelligence and test their theories. We can say that the only difference between our psychonauts and conventional scientists is that they apply their analytical and intuitive skills to the inner world, not the outer one. In this they have much in common with the spirit of Husserl's phenomenology, which aims for a detailed descriptive account of experience, putting aside any assumptions about its 'truth' or 'reality'.

Given this, it may not be surprising that one of the people in the modern world most responsible for arguing the case for imagination as a way of knowledge, and not merely as a means of 'make believe', spent a good part of his career as a phenomenologist, and in a sense remained one throughout it.

Henry Corbin was born in Paris in 1903. At the age of twelve he entered the Monastery School of St Maur. Ill-health plagued him in his early years, causing many absences from school, but by 1925 he had earned a degree in philosophy from the University of Paris, where he had studied under the philosopher and medieval scholar Étienne Gilson. Gilson brought the world of medieval philosophy to life for Corbin, presenting it, not as some dusty item in 'the cabinet of the history of philosophy', but as a tradition of 'permanent living possibilities of thought'.[14] This is much the same way in which Corbin himself would present to modern readers other living thought of the past.

It was through Gilson that Corbin was first introduced to Arab philosophy, specifically the work of Avicenna (980–1030), who taught a version of Aristotle informed by the ideas of Neoplatonism.

This had reached the Arab world following the 'esoteric exodus' from ancient Alexandria.[15] But it was while studying Stoicism and St Augustine at the École des Hautes Études that Corbin encountered a thinker who would change his life. Louis Massignon, the Catholic scholar of Islam and a vocal advocate of Christian-Muslim tolerance and understanding, gave Corbin a copy of an unusual text. It was the *Hikmat al Ishrak* – translated as *Oriental Philosophy* – of the Persian gnostic philosopher Suhrawardi, who was martyred for his beliefs in Aleppo in 1191 by order of Saladin. There was, Massignon thought, 'something in it', for Corbin. He was right. The encounter was decisive. In an interview years later Corbin explained that 'with my meeting with Suhrawardi my spiritual destiny ... was sealed. His Platonism, expressed in terms of Zoroastrian and ancient Persian angelology, illuminated the path that I was seeking'.[16]

That path, though, would lead through phenomenology, or at least the version of it presented by Husserl's one-time friend but later philosophical opponent, Martin Heidegger. In 1930 Corbin began reading Heidegger and in 1931 he travelled to Freiburg, where Heidegger had taken over Husserl's professorship following his retirement in 1928. The meeting proved fruitful and there were further encounters in 1935 and 1936. In 1938 a selection of Heidegger's essays Corbin had translated into French appeared under the title *Que'est-ce que c'est la Métaphysique?*, Heidegger's introduction to French readers. Corbin's translations had a profound effect on the French philosophical scene and were read avidly by people like Jean-Paul Sartre and Maurice Merleau-Ponty, major figures in existentialism.[17] It was also around this time that Corbin developed a close friendship with the Christian existential philosopher Nikolai Berdyaev, who had been expelled from Leninist Russia and had found a home in Paris. Berdyaev, too, was a prophet of the imagination, and his early work, *The Meaning of the Creative Act* (1916) remains a thrilling exploration of the spiritual character of creativity. It was during this time too that Corbin started attending the famous Eranos Conferences held in Ascona, Switzerland, where he became friends and colleagues with Jung and other esoteric scholars.

Corbin was taken with Heidegger's notion of truth as *aletheia*, as a 'revealing', a 'letting be shown'.[18] *Aletheia* is an ancient Greek word meaning 'disclosure' or 'unconcealedness'. Heidegger traced the word 'phenomenon' to the ancient Greek *phainesthai,* meaning 'that which shows itself in the light'. This was in opposition to Kant's belief that phenomena were representations that our cognitive apparatus makes of the *verboten* 'thing-in-itself' – thus opening a divide between knowledge and being – and positivism's idea of truth as scientific fact expressed in logical propositions – so reducing truth to the limits of banal prose. Yet while phenomena disclosed themselves in *aletheia* they at the same time concealed themselves; they remained question marks, pointing to the revelation of Being. It was through Heidegger's emphasis on the work of seeing 'what was hidden in plain sight', as it were – and we remember Goethe's remark that Nature is given in her totality if we have the eyes to see it – that his phenomenology moved toward interpretation and, eventually, to hermeneutics, the study of how we understand things.

Hermeneutics would, in the end, become the central theme of Corbin's work. He would find much to lead him there in the obscure but profoundly stimulating writings of the eighteenth century 'anti-Enlightenment' thinker Johann Georg Hamann, 'the Magus of the North', as the philosopher Isaiah Berlin called him.[19] Hamann was a kind of *éminence grise* of Romanticism. A friend of Kant's, and extolled by Goethe, Hegel and Kierkegaard, Hamann began as a true believer in the Enlightenment, but at some point he lost faith in reason and science as the royal roads to truth and knowledge. Where the Enlightenment saw these as absolutely fundamental in our attempt to understand the world, Hamann argued that they rested on an a-rational, pre-logical faith, rooted in the imagination and determined by the mysterious ways of language, which reason and logic will never grasp as they themselves emerge from it.

With Owen Barfield and Erich Heller, Hamann agreed that 'poetry is the mother-tongue of the human race', and that we have 'fallen' from this in our fascination with logical deduction and scientific explanation.[20] Like Barfield, Hamann believed that at the earliest time, the split between word and thing that we experience today – with words as arbitrary 'signifiers' pointing to an equally arbitrary 'signified' – was not the case. He posited a pre-lapsarian, Edenic language in which 'creature spoke to creature' because all shared in the *logos* of the Creator.

For the *Sprachphilosoph* George Steiner, Hamann's work is 'radiantly dark' and springs 'from the pregnant muddle of his extraordinary intellect and his intimacy with theosophical and Kabbalistic speculations'.[21] Like the Kabbalists, Hamann believed that language, the word, was at the very heart of existence. For Hamann, language is not a rational system of notation, devised to communicate information, but the very stuff of being. For him, in the beginning was the word, literally. He works toward a 'general theory of significant signs' under the assumption that 'a nerve fabric of secret meanings and revelations lies below the surface structure of all language'.[22] We decipher when we read, turning black squiggles on a page into meaningful content, but also when we observe Nature, which is a script written by God for his creatures to interpret in order to share in its hidden meaning. The philosopher of symbolism, Ernst Cassirer, agrees with Steiner. As Cassirer wrote, for Hamann, language 'is not a collection of discursive conventional signs for discursive concepts, but is the symbol and counterpart of the same divine life which everywhere surrounds us visibly and invisibly, mysteriously yet revealingly'.[23]

It was this notion, that signs of the divine hand behind creation surround us, if only we can learn the secret of how to read them, that led Corbin to plunge into the difficult practice of what he called 'spiritual hermeneutics', the art, we can say, of deciphering God's handwriting. Corbin referred to this using the Arabic term *ta'wil,* a hermeneutical practice that shares much with Goethe's 'active seeing', Schwaller de Lubicz's 'intelligence of the heart', and Barfield's 'participation'. In essence it is a means of 'looking through' phenomena, making them translucent, penetrating their surface – without discarding it – in order to perceive their depths, their interior. If phenomena simultaneously conceal and reveal a hidden, occult reality, then *ta'wil* is the interpretative method by which that occult reality is revealed, by returning its apparent surface, what is known as *zahir,* to its true depths, known as *batin.*

But if Hamann and Heidegger provided the philosophical impetus for Corbin's work, it was Suhrawardi who spoke to his mystical longing, which ran deep in him. Corbin's mysticism, we can say, was one of listening, of being attentive to 'things' so as to hear their voice. In 1932 Corbin expressed this in a piece of meditative writing composed near Lake Siljan in Sweden. In 'Theology by the Lakeside' Corbin reflected that: 'There is only revelation' and that 'things will tell you who they are, if you listen, surrendered to them, like a lover'. (We remember Goethe's 'affectionate' attention to his plants and Max Scheler's notion of 'phenomenological love'.) Corbin says that things will speak to him because, in the peace of the northern forest, the Earth came to him as an Angel – rather as Gustav Fechner had perceived it following his illumination. 'For at each moment that you really read ... that you listen to the Angel, and to the Earth, and to Woman, you receive Everything'. But when we try to understand such gifts with the logical mind, 'give a name and retain, explain and recover, ah! there remains but a cipher ...'[24] Knowledge, then, is something more than the literal facts of experience recounted accurately. What we truly know is only what we suffer in our own being. Once again, only like can know like.

The need for a change of being in order to receive certain kinds of knowledge is at the heart of the 'angelised Platonism' Corbin found in Suhrawardi. Suhrawardi was born in 1155 near the present-day towns of Zanjan and Bijar Garrus in northwest Iran; he is named after his birthplace, Suhraward. After studying Aristotle and Avicenna in Maragheh and then logic in Isfahan, Suhrawardi embarked on a 'knowledge quest' or 'initiatory journey', a not unfamiliar activity for esoteric scholars. This took him through Anatolia, where he came into contact with Sufi schools and masters, including Fakhr al-Din al-Mardini. Like Suhrawardi himself, Fakhr al-Din al-Mardini combined mysticism with rigorous logic, a union that Suhrawardi looked for in other seekers of truth. Suhrawardi adopted the Sufic way of life, embracing an ascetic practice, wearing the rough *suf* wool, from which the Sufis get their name and surrendering himself to the ecstasies of *sama,* the Sufi music. But he also maintained a strict philosophical discipline, subjecting his ecstasies to severe criticism and analysis. His work was 'addressed precisely to those who aspire at once to both mystical experience and philosophical knowledge' and should, he said, be transmitted only to 'him who is worthy, chosen from among those who have given evidence of a solid knowledge of the peripaticians' philosophy [Aristotle] while their hearts are nevertheless captured by love for the divine Light'.[25] It was clear to Suhrawardi, as it was to other 'imaginative knowers', that what was needed in order to arrive at real 'truth', was thought and feeling working together in a creative polarity, not in opposition.

Suhrawardi reached Aleppo in 1183 and he soon became friends with the city's governor, al-Malik al-Zahir, the son of the great Salah ad-Din Yusuf Ibn Ayyub, known to the west as Saladin. Suhrawardi became al-Mailk's tutor, a position envied by the local scholars, who already scorned Suhrawardi because of his heretical beliefs and skill in dialectics, which he displayed to their regret in their debates with him. He was obviously influenced by the words of the 'philosophers', which for devout Muslims was a term of abuse. Soon the scholars' enmity toward Suhrawardi would prove fatal.

The philosophers who influenced Suhrawardi came from pre-Islamic Persia, ancient Greece and Egypt. Together their ideas formed a potent blend of Zoroastrianism, Plato and the wisdom traditions of Alexandria, what Suhrawardi called a 'philosophy of Light', a tradition of esoteric metaphysics that was handed down from sage to sage, Suhrawardi believed, through the ages. In 1186 Suhrawardi tried to capture its essence in *Hikmat al-Ishraq*, translated, as mentioned, as *Oriental Philosophy* and also as *The Philosophy of Illumination*, the book that set Corbin on his hermeneutical quest. Suhrawardi wrote of an initiatic chain, a school of adepts reaching back into the dim past, and which included the fabled Hermes Trismegistus, Zoroaster, Pythagoras, Plato, Plotinus and others. All were informed by the same primal revelation, the *prisca theologia* or 'primal theology', which it was his task to resurrect.

These ideas did not go down well with the orthodox jurists, *ulama* and mullahs of Aleppo. They accused Suhrawardi of practising magic and prophecy, and said he would lead the people and their governor, Saladin's son, astray. They petitioned Saladin for Suhrawardi's execution saying he was corrupting the young, the same charge that the council of Athens had brought against Socrates. Saladin accepted their petition and ordered Suhrawardi's death.

Suhrawardi voiced a spirited defence and al-Malik al-Zahir at first refused to carry out his father's command, but eventually he had to concede. It remains unclear exactly how Suhrawardi met his death; some accounts say he was starved to death, others say he was strangled, still others say he was beheaded or crucified. But sometime in 1191 – some accounts put the date further on – Suhrawardi died. Henceforth he was known, not only as the Shaikh al-Ishraq, the 'Master of Illumination', but also as the Shaikh al-Maqtl, the 'murdered Master'.

If Suhrawardi's mission was to resurrect the ancient philosophy of Light, we can see Corbin's own mission as carrying on Suhrawardi's work in the modern world. Through his many writings Corbin has introduced modern readers to an idea that runs throughout esoteric thought, although articulated in different ways, and which we've already touched on a few times in this book.[26] This is what is known as the *'àlam al-mithâl,* or, as Corbin calls it, the *mundus imaginalis,* or 'Imaginal World'. As Corbin writes, this is 'a very precise order of reality, which corresponds to a precise mode of perception'. This 'order of reality' and 'mode of perception' is based on a 'visionary spiritual experience' that Suhrawardi believed was 'as fully relevant as the observations of Hipparchus and Ptolemy are considered to be relevant to astronomy'.[27]

Hipparchus and Ptolemy may no longer be so relevant to contemporary astronomy, but Suhrawardi's point is clear. The 'visionary spiritual experience' he speaks of, which involves his 'inner firmament', is, for the gnostic philosopher, the equivalent of the meticulous observations and charts the astronomers of his time made of the stars, our 'outer firmament'. But while Hipparchus, Ptolemy and today's astronomers use their eyes to make their observations, Suhrawardi's account of his experience is based on the use of his organs of inner sight. What these inner organs perceive is just as 'real' as the stars that Hipparchus charted, but like the inhabitants of Jung's 'objective psyche', or those of Huxley's 'Mind at Large', it exists in an interior dimension that we can gain access to through our subjective worlds.

Corbin coined the term 'Imaginal' for this realm, in order to differentiate it from our usual ideas of the 'imaginary', and he placed it in an intermediate sphere between the realm of pure ideas –

Plato's Forms – and that of sensory reality, solid matter. He affirmed that the Imaginal is 'ontologically as real as the world of the senses and that of the intellect'.[28] This means that the Imaginal has its own mode of being, and that it can't be reduced to the status of 'just an idea' – as Schiller considered Goethe's Primal Plant – or some reflection of a physical tree. We can think of the idea of a 'tree' and know what we mean by it. And we can also see an actual, physical tree, standing in the garden. But we can also imagine a tree and form an image of it in our minds. This image occupies a kind of middle ground between the bare notion of 'tree' and the physical thing rising up from the lawn, rather as an artist's image of what he wants to express occupies a middle ground between the idea behind his work and the finished, physical product. The 'blank slate' school of psychology says that our image of a tree is merely the mental residue of our seeing an actual tree. Goethe would disagree. He would say that our image of a tree is an expression of the *Urpflanze,* which has a reality of its own, not dependent upon information about trees given by the senses collecting in my mind. As Goethe said, without this prior image, how would I know what was a tree and what wasn't?

We usually think of the imaginary as unreal, false – in general as some way less than the physical, sensory world. Or we see it as leading to 'novelty' or the 'cutting edge' in some process – this means technology most often today. But Corbin and Jung and others contend that for them – and potentially for all of us – the 'Imaginal' constitutes an entire world of its own, that is just as objective as the sensory world, with its own geography, history, laws, and, as Jung discovered, its own inhabitants.

Suhrawardi discovered some inhabitants of the *mundus imaginalis* himself. His need for a 'precise mode of perception' arose from the kinds of initiatory experiences he underwent and which led to his 'philosophy of illumination'. Through a series of meditations, Suhrawardi charted the way within. His inner voyage led to what he called *Nâ-Kojâ-Abâd,* 'the country of no-where'. Unlike Utopia, this did not mean a place that does not exist – a distinction Corbin is at pains to make. Rather it indicates an interior location, a place that cannot be found on any map, or any physical terrain, but which occupies a position in Suhrawardi's 'hierarchy of light'. This is the chain of being reaching from the highest spiritual realms to our own mundane world, versions of which appear in Hermeticism, Neoplatonism, Kabbalah and other traditions of Western esotericism. This descent marks an increasing solidification or materialisation of what is in essence spiritual; that is, non-manifest, non-physical.

For Suhrawardi, borrowing from Neoplatonic ontology, light is the closest we come in the physical world to the non-manifest spiritual essence. From a Supreme Light of Lights, beyond our physical world, emanations radiate out, gradually 'hardening', and becoming dense – an idea that modern science seems to have picked up on – and in the process eventually arriving at our universe.[29]

Suhrawardi sees this 'ladder of lights' as an angelic hierarchy, a theme he borrows from Zoroastrianism. In this arrangement, each rung on the ladder is an angel, while the angel itself is the state of consciousness proper to this level of being. As in Hermeticism, Neoplatonism, Gnosticism and Kabbalah, in Suhrawardi's 'philosophy of light', the philosopher's task is to journey back up the ladder, to ascend it to its source. This was accomplished through a series of meditations and visualisations in which, as Jung did, the philosopher would encounter some of the inhabitants of this strange realm.

Suhrawardi wrote what we can call 'visionary tales' in which the states of consciousness – or levels of being – that he reached would be symbolised in a narrative, with the characters and setting embodying the spiritual realities he encountered. That is, he used his imagination to transmute his 'inner spiritual states' into 'vision events', creating a kind of story symbolising his level of consciousness.[30] We can say he engaged in what we can call a kind of 'waking dream', precisely the kind of conscious fantasy that enabled Jung to pass out of his everyday world and into the 'objective psyche'. Jung later called his method of doing this 'active imagination', a means of reaching a creative dialogue between the conscious and unconscious mind which he often used in his practice.[31] That Corbin would agree with the idea that the Imaginal can be reached via a ' waking dream' is clear. He urged his readers that we needed 'to be clear in our minds as to the real meaning and impact of the mass of information about the typographies explored in the visionary state, i.e., the intermediary state between sleeping and waking'.[32]

This liminal condition is known as the 'hypnagogic state', a transitional mode of consciousness that we experience at least twice a day: when we fall asleep and when we wake up.[33] As I have pointed out elsewhere, Jung was an experienced hypnagogist, as was Swedenborg.[34] Swedenborg was apparently able to maintain the liminal state between sleeping and waking for extended periods and it was during these that he undertook his journeys to heaven and hell.[35] Swedenborg's visits to heaven, hell, and an intermediary sphere he called the 'spirit world' were undertaken by him in the same way as Suhrawardi undertook his journey to *Nâ-Kojâ-Abâd*. He would relax into a condition he called 'passive potency', a state of observant receptivity, a kind of calm alertness, in which his conscious mind could watch the operations of the unconscious – or, as Swedenborg would have said it, the spiritual worlds. This was not far different from Goethe's attitude toward his Primal Plant with his 'active seeing'. Swedenborg would then be taken on a tour of heaven, hell, or the spirit world by an angel, rather as Jung was shown around the collective unconscious by Philemon. What made this different from a dream is that Swedenborg remained conscious throughout; he 'saw' and 'heard' in the same way that he did in waking life, but what he observed took place within him.[36]

Movement in these other spheres, as in *Nâ-Kojâ-Abâd,* was not through a physical space, but through changes of 'state', changes in consciousness, so 'place' and 'state' became synonymous. While many of his contemporaries still believed in an actual heaven or hell occupying some remote yet nevertheless tangible place, Swedenborg was advancing the very modern idea that heaven and hell are states of mind, dispositions of the soul, interior spaces that we carry around with us. As Swedenborg and other explorers of the hypnagogic have observed, the visions seen in this state are self-symbolic. That is, the images seen and voices heard in the hypnagogic state symbolise the state of the psyche at that time. Herbert Silberer, a colleague of Jung and, like him, deeply interested in the link between alchemy and psychology, wrote an important paper on this phenomena which almost certainly influenced Jung's ideas about 'active imagination'. It is not a far cry from the auto-symbolic character of hypnagogic phenomena to Suhrawardi's use of the imagination to transform 'inner states' into 'vision events'.[37]

Another area in which Swedenborg and Suhrawardi meet is in Swedenborg's notion of the 'doctrine of correspondences'.[38] This states that there is a correspondence between the things of the earth and those of the spiritual realms. Everything in our world of space and time corresponds to a spiritual reality in the realms beyond. 'The whole natural world,' Swedenborg wrote, 'corresponds to the spiritual world – not just the natural world in general, but actually in details. It is vital,' he tells us, 'to understand that the natural world emerges and endures from the spiritual world, just like an effect from the cause that produces it'.[39] Spiritual knowledge, spiritual education, comes from the slow process of learning how to decipher these correspondences, to see the reflection of the higher in the lower, the divine in the everyday. Just as the reader must interpret a text, we read the world, trying to grasp the deeper meaning below the literal one; as the Nobel prize winning poet Czeslaw Milosz said: 'Swedenborg's world is all language'.[40]

The similarity of the practice of recognising correspondences to *ta'wil* seems obvious. Both are a form of 'spiritual hermeneutics', the discipline of divining the hidden meaning, the depth *(batin* or esoteric) both announced and obscured by the surface *(zahir* or exoteric)*. As Christopher Bamford writes, for both Suhrawardi and Swedenborg 'there is no apparent, sensible phenomenon that does not also mask, and hence manifest, a hidden, suprasensible noumenal reality'.[41] In the nineteenth century, the French poet Charles Baudelaire, a reader of Swedenborg, took his notion of correspondences and applied it to poetry and art in general, in the process inaugurating the age of Symbolism, which looked at the world metaphorically, in ways that link it to Barfield's ideas about participation and Heller's reservations about the 'age of prose'.[42]

I should mention that Rudolf Steiner was also an accomplished hypnagogist, and there is good reason to believe that when Steiner read the Akashic Record, the occult history of the cosmos that he was able to discern 'supersensibly', he did this when in the hypnagogic state. Accounts of his lectures suggest that when Steiner read the Akashic Record, he would turn his eyes away from the light, retreat into himself, and make a 'deliberate adjustment of his being', and that when he spoke about ancient Atlantis, Lemuria, or some other aspect of the occult history of humankind or the earth, he seemed to be actually seeing what he was conveying to his audience.[43] Steiner believed that prior to the kind of consciousness common to us now, humankind experienced a kind of 'picture thinking', rather like the poetical condition of things Owen Barfield suggested was the case before the rise of independent rational thought. Steiner called this ancient form of consciousness by the somewhat awkward term 'Old Moon' and in *A Secret History of Consciousness* I suggest that there are important similarities between our Old Moon consciousness and the hypnagogic state.

Jung visited the objective psyche, Swedenborg went to heaven and hell, Steiner read the Akashic Record. In Suhrawardi's case his journey to *Nâ-Kojâ-Abâd* entailed its own unique and equally unusual features. Although his 'visionary tales', and those of other 'philosophers of light' that Corbin studied, differ in detail, they all share some elements in common. When, like the others, Suhrawardi had entered the proper state of calm alertness, his attention focused within, the interior voyage began. As Jung and Swedenborg did, Suhrawardi soon found that he was not alone. He discovered he was in the presence of a spiritual being. This being, known as 'the messenger', asks the voyager, Suhrawardi himself, who is called 'the stranger', who he is and where he comes from. The stranger answers that he is a traveller who seeks to return home, to his true country beyond the realm of the senses. The journey homeward will take him beyond Mount Qâf, what Corbin calls the 'cosmic mountain'. This is made up of the celestial spheres the voyager must ascend on his return journey up the ladder of light back to his source, a common theme in the Western inner tradition. There, beyond Mount Qâf, the voyager finds his true self, his higher being, and as he does he finds that he is approaching *Hūrqalyā*, the 'spiritual city', which begins at the 'convex surface' of the 'Ninth Sphere', the 'Sphere of Spheres', which embraces the entire cosmos.

The stranger then passes beyond this sphere, and when he does, something extraordinary happens. Where in our everyday world we assume that we are 'in' the cosmos – that like everything else we are 'objects' situated in space – here, beyond Mount Qâf, this seems to be no longer the case. Here, what we experience and perceive as the 'outer world' is seen to exist entirely within our own inner world. We are not in the cosmos; it is within us, something the ancient Hermeticists, with their notion of the microcosm, or little cosmos, understood. As Corbin writes: 'once the journey is completed, the reality which has hitherto been an inner and hidden one turns out to envelop, surround or contain that which at first was outer and visible'.[44]

This seems a somewhat mystical or esoteric way of expressing Husserl's idea of stepping outside the 'natural standpoint', something Corbin would have been familiar with from his phenomenological studies. Certainly the most fundamental matter-of-fact truth of the natural standpoint is that the world exists outside us, and has done so, for aeons before we existed and will do so for aeons after we die. Stepping outside the natural standpoint entails a temporary suspension of this belief, but for those who arrive beyond the Ninth Sphere it strikes as a revelation. As Corbin wrote: 'for those who reach *Nâ-Kojâ-Abâd* everything happens contrary to the evidence of ordinary consciousness …'[45] In Suhrawardi's case, and in that of the other gnostic voyagers who followed in his path, the reality of a cosmos inside our consciousness is brought home with a peculiar power.

Corbin was aware of the question asked earlier, of how inner voyagers, travellers in the Imaginal, can navigate among the rocks and shallows of fantasy and on to the wider waters of the true imagination, the *imaginatio vera,* or *astrum in homine,* Paracelsus' 'inner firmament'. There is a 'lost continent of the mind', but the way to rediscovering it requires accurate maps and charts and the knowledge necessary to read them. Corbin speaks of a 'type of control' that can 'protect imagination from straying and from reckless wastage'. We can know when imagination has gone astray because at that point it will 'cease to fulfil its function of perceiving and producing the symbols that lead to inner intelligence'. At that point it will have left the *mundus imaginalis* and have entered realms of subjective fantasy.[46]

What differentiates the images seen with true imagination from the phantasmagoria of subjective fantasy is that the phenomena of the Imaginal have the power to dispel 'the mutual isolation of consciousness and its object, of thought and being'. That is to say, their reality and our knowing them, our experience of them, are the same. As Corbin says, with this 'phenomenology becomes ontology', 'appearance' and 'being' becoming one.[47] The split between reality and our knowledge of it, which has held Western philosophy in thrall, is healed.

For Westerners, brought up with the unquestioned acceptance of a strict distance between subject and object, this is not an easy thing to grasp, and Corbin's meaning is not always clear. But with persistent meditation it gets through. For example, the following reflection I believe requires repeated reading. 'The soul,' Corbin writes, is 'capable of perceiving concrete things whose existence ... constitutes *eo ipso* the very concrete existential form of these things'. That is to say, with these phenomena 'consciousness and its object are ontologically inseparable'. In the Imaginal, knower and known are one. The kinds of phenomena we find in the Imaginal are what Goethe meant by his *Urphänomena*. For Goethe and Corbin they are both 'unconditional and irreducible' and 'cannot manifest in any other way in this world'.

This is what Goethe meant when he told his friend Herder that with the secret of the Primal Plant, 'it will be possible to go on forever inventing plants and know that their existence is logical' because they would not be 'the shadowy phantoms of vain imagination, but possess an inner necessity and truth'.[48] This inner necessity and truth keeps the imagination from sliding off the rails.

It is through the work of the 'active' or 'true imagination' that, as Corbin writes, 'psychic energies that have been neglected or paralysed by our habits' can be revived'.[49] These energies can then be used to perform the work of *ta'wil,* the spiritual hermeneutics that can resuscitate the world of phenomena, which has fallen into the deadening embrace of mechanistic science and utilitarian exploitation. Functioning as a 'faculty and organ of knowledge, just as real – if not more real than – the senses', 'true imagination' releases 'things' from their bondage by returning them to their archetypal source in the Imaginal. At the same time true imagination can free us from what Barfield calls our 'idolatry' to things, our slavish deference to their presumed primacy over the consciousness that co-creates them, a mistaken humbleness abetted by reductionist science and 'blank slate' psychology. True imagination has a transformative power; it can alchemically transmute information from the senses into symbols to be deciphered or language to be translated. In essence it turns 'facts' into 'meaning' by linking parts into wholes. It does not 'construct something unreal' – that is the business of fantasy – but 'unveils the hidden reality'. Its work, as Corbin writes, is to 'occultate the apparent' – that is to obscure it – and it does this in order to 'manifest the hidden', turning, we can say, the inside out.[50]

As Owen Barfield did, Corbin recognised the need for a 'responsibility of the imagination', guidelines as it were to keep it from, as he says, straying into 'reckless wastefulness'. For Corbin this meant a tradition, a body of practices and beliefs that recognised the importance of the imagination and could provide a structure and discipline that would help it keep its integrity. As a 'philosopher of light', he understood this in a particular way. He spoke of the need for 'access to a cosmology structured similarly to that of the traditional oriental philosophies, with a plurality of universes arranged in ascending order'.[51] By this he meant the ladder of being that is at the heart of the Western esoteric tradition, the order of reality reaching from the unmanifest source to the solid earth, that Hermeticists, Neoplatonists and Kabbalists all in different ways recognise. Traditional oriental philosophies meant for Corbin the 'philosophy of light' and *prisca theologia* that Suhrawardi wanted to resurrect, but we would not do wrong if we broadened this to include all philosophies that set mind, spirit or consciousness as primary, rather than give physical reality pride of place, as our scientist faiths do.

Such a tradition is needed, Corbin believed, because without it there is the very real danger that in its absence, our imagination will remain, as he puts it, 'out of focus' and its 'recurrent conjunctions with our will-to-power will be a never-ending source of horrors'.[52] A wilful imagination can be a formidable thing. That the collective imagination was clearly out of focus seemed obvious to Corbin when he wrote these words some forty years ago, and it is questionable whether it has righted itself in the meantime. Indeed there is evidence to suggest that it has got worse. Corbin even entertained the idea that it may have been in some way necessary to lose access to the *mundus imaginalis,* to allow it to be bereft of its sacred character and become secularised, so that the 'fantastic, the horrible, the monstrous, the macabre, the miserable, and the absurd could come to the fore'.[53] The similarity with Barfield's concern about an unchecked imagination – or, more accurately, fantasy – producing a 'fantastically hideous world' seems obvious. Perhaps by allowing it *carte blanche* the unconscious might be purged of its demons; it could exhaust its shadow by allowing it free reign, and through indulgence reach satiety if not wisdom. The blasé acceptance of the surfeit of sex, violence, vulgarity and coarse, crude humour which makes up much of contemporary entertainment – and of which there seems no end – suggests at least that our unregulated imaginations have run out of steam. This may lead to a change of taste, or, perhaps more likely, to the need for stronger stimulants to elicit some reaction.

Yet if such an inoculation of the hideous was in some way necessary, surely by now we have endured its effects long enough to gain whatever benefit was expected from it? Is it not time for the imagination to remember its true calling, its real work and purpose? There have been many who believed this was so and who throughout the Imaginal's decline into the merely imaginary, worked to keep the tradition of the true imagination alive. They understood the need for a 'plurality of universes arranged in ascending order', for a hierarchy of spiritual states and conditions of consciousness, because it was evident to them that reality itself was so arranged and that ultimately the mind behind this arrangement was one with their own. Like Suhrawardi and other ancient philosophers of light, they felt themselves exiled in this fallen world and sought the way back home. For many of them that way led through poetry.

Chapter Five
The Learning of the Imagination

Henry Corbin was not the only one concerned that a loss of true imagination could lead to a fascination with the 'fantastic, the horrible, the monstrous, and the absurd'. Erich Kahler was one of the leading lights of a generation of Central European humanist scholars the like of which is practically unknown today; George Steiner is perhaps the closest we can get to one of them. Along with many other Central European intellectuals, Kahler fled the rise of Nazism in the 1930s and found a new home in the United States. In Kahler's case, this meant Princeton, New Jersey.

At the time of Kahler's arrival in 1938 – following some time in Great Britain – Princeton was home to perhaps the most famous of the intellectual émigrés fleeing fascism, Albert Einstein. Kahler and Einstein became friends, and remained so until Einstein's death in 1955. Kahler was also a close friend of the novelist Thomas Mann, whose books, like Einstein's, were heaped upon the bonfires by ardent members of the German Student Union in universities across the Third Reich. Another novelist who became close friends with Kahler, and who was also persecuted by the Nazis, was the Austrian Hermann Broch. It was in Kahler's home in Princeton that Broch wrote what is considered to be his masterpiece, *The Death of Virgil*, a work that is as much a gigantic prose poem as it is a novel, depicting in hallucinatory detail the consciousness of the Roman poet Virgil as he approaches death. In the process Broch created literature that, as Aldous Huxley remarked, brought the reader to 'the very limits of the expressible'.

'The limits of the expressible' may be an appropriate way to encapsulate the theme of a series of lectures Kahler gave in spring 1967, at Princeton University, just three years before his death in 1970. The title of his lectures, *The Disintegration of Form in the Arts*, may give us an idea of what Kahler was concerned with. What troubled him was what he saw as the seemingly irrevocable 'loss of form' in the arts. This may seem of limited interest, of significance only to students of art history. But like Corbin and Barfield, Kahler saw the state of the imagination in the late twentieth century as an indication of wider issues. Like them, Kahler took what was happening in the world of art as a sign of certain troubling developments in Western civilisation, but also as an agent of what he considered 'an extremely dangerous trend of events'.[1]

By the time Kahler gave his lectures, Western art had for some years gone through a series of dizzying changes and for a humanist of his generation it would not be an exaggeration to say that it had become something unrecognisable. Exactly where we want to mark the start of this change is debatable, but I think we can agree that between Marcel Duchamp's urinal and Andy Warhol's Brillo box, art had entered terrain rather different from the kind it had inhabited before. Kahler had lived through this transformation and seen it all and his response to art's 'loss of form' couldn't be dismissed as the whinging of an old fogey, out of step with the times. Hermann Broch's work was considered as 'experimental' as that of James Joyce – whose *Ulysses* was like nothing before it – and Einstein had already caused a revolution in our ideas about the universe. Kahler, who knew both men well, was intimately acquainted with innovation, both in the arts and in science.

It was the times themselves, from Kahler's perspective, that were very much out of step, at least from the point of view of someone who was concerned with 'what makes human beings human, what keeps humanity, the *genus humanum* human'.[2] The loss of form that troubled Kahler was responsible for more than a glut of bad, or at best incomprehensible art, reprehensible and disturbing as that was. It was a sign that our very idea of what it means to be human was under attack.

Form, for Kahler, is a sign of wholeness, of a coherence between self and the world, of an 'inner organisation' that is necessary and not arbitrary, an idea we have already looked at in different ways in this book. It is not the same as shape. A lake, he argues, has a shape, but as it lacks structure, it has no form; water, we know, takes on the shape of its container, and if the shoreline around a lake was to change, the shape of the lake would too. It has no organic wholeness, hence no organic form. The same is true of a stone. If you split a stone in two, you do not have two halves of one broken whole but only two smaller stones.[3] 'But,' as Kahler writes, 'any organic body, any living creature has form, indeed *is* form', a remark with which Goethe would have been in total agreement.[4]

Form and its metamorphosis were, we know, of central importance to Goethe. He would recognise, as we all would, that if you cut a plant in half, you do not have two smaller plants but one dead one. Given that humans, for Kahler, are 'up to this point the most highly structured being', we are, then, the 'most advanced natural form of all'. This is because human reality 'extends far beyond physical existence into realms of psychic, intellectual, and spiritual reflection' and 'through memory and awareness of identity, into the dimension of time, that is, into history'.[5] Human form, then, is not only limited to that of our physical bodies, but involves our entire idea and significance of what it means to be human.

Form, for Kahler, as it was for Goethe, is not static. He was not arguing for some fixed idea of humanity, to be maintained against all change. 'Whenever new spheres, new depths of existence are disclosed by a thrust into the unknown,' he writes, 'these experiences will have to be integrated into a further complete whole' which can lead to a 'broader, more comprehensive, perfection of form'. 'Again and again the wholeness of existence must be re-established, a new, wider and more complex wholeness must be apprehended'.[6] This effort entails the 'intense rendering of some existential coherence' which, ultimately, should lead to an increase in consciousness.

Consciousness, for Kahler, is defined as 'awareness of self' and of 'the coherence of the self within a coherence of its surrounding world'.[7] Yet what Kahler saw taking place in the twentieth century was the opposite of this. Instead of an increase in consciousness through the assimilation of experience into a greater whole, what was taking place seemed to be an unstoppable 'erosion' of such awareness.

Beginning with Dada and moving through Surrealism up to abstract expressionism, 'action painting', and the 'happenings' of the 1960s, what Kahler saw was 'the total *destruction of coherence, and with it … the conscious destruction of consciousness'*. It was an eruption of purposeful chaos, we might say. Looking out on the landscape of modern art and culture, Kahler saw an 'outspoken attempt to produce incoherence as such, devoid of any cause or purpose'. There was a 'veritable cult of incoherence, of sheer senselessness and aimlessness'.[8] In the aleatory compositions of John Cage, the 'active confusion' of the intellectual demagogue, Marshall McLuhan, who abandoned meaningful content with his dictum that the 'medium was the message', and the sensory barrage of 'multi-media' overload – siphoning off aspects of 'Scientism' for artistic purposes – Kahler saw at work a deliberate attempt to undermine the whole conception of coherence in a misguided movement to break free of what it considered the restrictions of outworn, outmoded sensibilities. One of the main driving forces behind this demolition work, Kahler believed, was the increasing technological character of modern life. Today mechanisation 'takes command' and grows and grows 'unimpeded, according to its own self-propelled rationale', pushing it more and more beyond our capacity to control it. The fear Goethe had about a kind of knowledge that would not lead to the good life but to what was pernicious seemed, to Kahler, to have been justified.

Kahler wasn't the only cultural commentator disturbed by developments in modern art and in culture at large. In the same year that Kahler gave his lectures the historian Jacques Barzun published an article in which he remarked on the 'now standardised virulence of the artistic temper, the desperate violence of expression resorted to as a matter of course'.[9] Barzun suggested that the reason for this *de rigueur* artistic violence – what Kahler called 'creative vandalism' – was the permissive society that arrived when the forces of Liberalism 'no longer found barriers to break down' and the 'last ounce of energy in emancipation' was gone. He quotes the existentialist writer Simone de Beauvoir, who said of her early years: 'We had no external limitations, no overriding authority, no imposed pattern of existence'.[10] Such freedom – if that is what it is – Barzun believed leaves 'nothing to push against but the empty air'. This seems agreeable at first but it soon 'ends by causing the anguish of pointlessness – the horror of the absurd'.[11] A few years later Barzun expanded on this theme in talks he gave for the A.W. Mellon Lectures in the Fine Arts, under the title *The Use and Abuse of Art*.[12]

Another voice concerned about what was happening to the modern imagination was that of William Barrett, an American philosopher whose book *Irrational Man,* published in 1958, was one of the first widely read popular works on existentialism. Barrett had a good grounding in the absurd but by the early 1970s, the forces of dissolution accompanying it seemed to have gotten out of hand. In a work called *Time of Need,* published in 1972, Barrett noted that 'the forms of imagination that any epoch produces are an ultimate datum on what that epoch is'.[13] If that was the case, then the epoch in question was something of a mess. Barrett echoed Kahler and Barzun by noting that 'an observer from outside might very well say of our art of the last fifty years that there seems let loose in it a rage to destroy, as if the culture itself were bent on working towards conclusions that destroy its own premises'.[14] But where Kahler and Barzun focused more on what was disturbing about recent developments, Barrett hit on an insight that Erich Heller had grasped as well.

One of the reasons for the chaos of modern culture, Barrett saw, was that the older, traditional symbols that once contained the poetic and aesthetic 'charge', had been emptied out. Like exhausted batteries, they could no longer hold the energy required to make an artistic impact, to move the viewer or to reveal new dimensions of reality. Through over exposure, a decline in religious and humanistic faith, the increasing mechanisation of life, or the growing cynicism of an audience who had seen it all and knew too much by half, the icons and images of an earlier tradition were now little more than clichés, old-fashioned targets on which the irony and sarcasm of the avant-garde scored repeated bullseyes. Duchamp's moustache on the *Mona Lisa* and Bunuel's film *L'Age d'Or* are prime examples, but one could easily provide many more.[15] This did not mean that the artist or poet found no new forms to hold the energies of art. But these now seemed haphazard and arbitrary, and in this he or she was spoiled for choice.

'Anything, and ever more *anything*', Heller said of the artist, 'invited his fair attention', turning him into 'the Don Juan of the creative spirit'.[16] Heller quotes from T.S. Eliot who asked: 'Why out of all we have heard, seen, felt … do certain images recur, charged with emotion, rather than others?' Eliot ran through a list of such images: 'the song of one bird, the leap of one fish, ... the scent of one flower, an old woman on a German mountain path...'[17] While in novelists like Proust, for whom a piece of cake opened inner doorways, or poets like Rilke, who offered his Angel simple, everyday things – a house, a bridge, a fountain or gate – what takes place is what the philosopher Arthur Danto called the 'transfiguration of the commonplace', in most other modern artistic expressions it is the commonplace that is emphasised and not the transfiguration.[18]

Someone who also recognised this draining of energy from hitherto traditional symbols and the rise of the commonplace, if not the brutal and ugly, was the poet and Blake scholar Kathleen Raine. Raine was born in 1908 in a suburb of London, but a move north took her from the grey streets of Ilford to a countryside still untamed by the modern world. In her early years she was taken to her grandparents' home where she roamed free amidst the beauty of nature and the years she spent on the Northumberland moors, on England's Scottish border, during the First World War, remained in her imagination as a kind of paradise, an Eden of delight:

> I lived in a world of flowers, minute but inexhaustible ...
> All were mine, whatever I saw was mine in the very act of
> seeing. To see was to know, to enter into total relationship
> with, to participate in the essential being of each *I am*.[19]

This time in nature taught her to see the world around her as a whole. 'Stream and rock, tree and fern, down to the most minute frond is formed each by the whole, and the whole by each'.[20] She knew that 'within that larger unity each centre of life unfolds its own unity of form in perfect and minute precision'.[21] With Erich Kahler and Goethe, Raine knew that 'the whole of organic life – the soul of nature – is engaged in nothing else but embodiment and unfolding of forms'. Even as a child she recognised that 'the whole is made up not of parts but of wholes'.[22]

This sense of wholeness, of coherence, of beauty manifesting in the forms of nature and finding its reflection in the soul, rooted itself in the young girl. Raine was so fascinated by the intricate and delicate forms of nature that when she arrived at Cambridge in 1926 she read sciences, botany and zoology. She had not given up her dream of being a poet. Her father, who was against the idea, was an English teacher with a great love of Shakespeare and Wordsworth, and along with nature her early years were filled with poetry and with old tales and legends of her mother's Scottish ancestry. Her mother encouraged her poetic ambitions, but at that time science offered a greater purchase on the difficult business of making a living than did the pursuit of the muse.

Her high school science teacher had impressed her with her passion for the subject, while Raine also felt that, although she loved it, she had no desire or need to be 'taught' literature. 'To be taught "about" literature,' she wrote, 'which is itself the teaching, seemed to me a waste of time'. It was there, in the books, to be read. Learning about the secret life of plants and the mysterious world of animals could not be done through books. And so she chose science, thereby making her father happy. But she had not abandoned poetry. Like Goethe, she did not see a necessary clash between the two.[23] For the time being science could provide an 'immediate delight', but her 'secret poetic vocation' had not vanished. She would merely keep it to herself.

Such secrecy proved necessary, and not only in order to mollify a concerned parent. Raine quickly discovered that while her friends and colleagues at Cambridge enjoyed reading, the kind of poetry that she loved and learned by heart was not their 'thing' at all. She herself looked in poetry 'for the sublime,' and in it 'listened for that resonance of "the eternal, in and through the temporal" of which Coleridge speaks'. But the world she was entering now had no place for the eternal; it was temporal, through and through, and acutely 'up to date'. It had no time for Coleridge, or her other favourites, Keats, Shelley, Yeats and Blake. The new friends she had made were all *au courant* with whatever was the fashionable thing, and the kind of poetry that made her heart leap with delight and remembrance was definitely not it. Aldous Huxley's acerbic novels, Ezra Pound's Imagism, the Bloomsbury world of Virginia Woolf, Lytton Strachey, Clive Bell and 'significant form'. It was a smart literary world informed with the new, anti-Romantic sentiment. Even a literary criticism all its own had grown up around it, the New Criticism of I.A. Richards, which was eager to mimic the scientistic exactitude of the latest philosophical fashion: logical positivism.

This ironically had grown out of the work of Ludwig Wittgenstein, who in his mystical *Tractatus Logico-Philosophicus* had come to the conclusion that 'what we cannot speak about we must pass over in silence', something with which Hermann Broch, who emerged from the same Vienna as Wittgenstein, would have agreed.[24] Broch and Wittgenstein both knew there was much of great, fundamental importance that could not be spoken about – in the explicit, fact-based language of the sciences, that is. But both also knew that in this ineffable sphere – what Francis Cornford called 'the vague'– lay all that was of meaning and significance in life. However, philosophers anxious to receive the kind of intellectual prestige increasingly accorded to scientists turned Wittgenstein on his head and took his admonition of silence to mean that whatever could not be spoken of with prosaic explicitness, was not only not worth trying to say, but absolutely meaningless.

Scientism and its missionaries had reached even poetry. That 'pernicious humanist "honesty" which mistrusts all knowledge but that of the senses', reigned supreme, and Raine felt she had to hide her true feelings so as to fit in.[25] 'The beauties' she had hitherto found in Milton and the Romantics 'were not of the imagination' – Corbin's *mundus imaginalis* – but were now seen as only 'imaginary', that is, false. Poetry must now 'conform to the new values of science'. It was a belief she could not fully embrace, although for a time she accepted that 'in discarding my own intuitions in order to learn a more "intelligent" way of reading poetry', she thought that she was 'taking the way from ignorance to knowledge'.[26]

She soon found that she had not, and had indeed achieved the opposite: a forgetting of the knowledge vouchsafed to those who remained for her the 'real poets'. The one poetic voice that reached her at this time did speak in the new, flat, prosaic manner, focusing on the banalities of life and alluding to some paradise that was indeed lost and irrevocably irrecoverable. But the unmistakable elegiac undertone and halting rhythms seemed appropriate. She came to feel that she, and her friends, did inhabit T.S. Eliot's *Waste Land*. But while the others somehow did not seem out of place in the bleak modern landscape, some remnant of Eden remained in her soul and made her an outsider.

It was not until sometime later that Raine published an essay that captured the essence of what she had worked to forget in those early Cambridge years, and the loss of which had, she believed, turned her Eden of delight into a barrenness. In 1967 a collection of Raine's essays entitled *Defending Ancient Springs* appeared. She had published poetry before this and in 1962 – a decade before Jacques Barzun – she had herself given the A.W. Mellon Foundation Lectures in Fine Art in Washington, D.C., on the subject of *Blake and Tradition*, later the title of her two volume critical *magnum opus*.[27] But *Defending Ancient Springs* was her first book of prose. And along with essays on Blake, Yeats, Coleridge and other poets, one work on a more general theme echoed in Raine's unmistakable way the concerns of Kahler, Barzun and – if the reader allows a certain temporal flexibility – Barrett.

'The Use of the Beautiful' voiced what the reader must assume were many of the hesitations Raine had overcome in order to swallow the 'technical literary talk' she had imbibed in Cambridge. The essay asked a simple question: what place did beauty have in modern culture? Raine's answer? Practically none. We live in a 'beautiless society', which for Raine was another way of saying that we lived in a culture that had lost its soul.[28]

As evidence of this Raine pointed to examples that would not have been out of place in the complaints of Kahler, Barzun, and Barrett. The fleeting and formless character of contemporary art had struck her too. She noted the 'instantaneous gesture which expresses finally nothing but its own instantaneity' and remarked that 'all images have dissolved into the flux of continuous transformation, so much so that form … can no longer be said to exist'.[29] She also felt the existential vacuum in which 'all becomes trivial, and nothing significant, since there is no standard by which anything could be called better or worse'.[30] The absurdity of it all was also apparent. 'The arts,' she wrote, 'have become the expression of the very incoherence and ignorance from which they normally provide release'.[31]

The arts, she argued, exist in order to provide such relief, or at least they used to, because it was their purpose to remind us of another order of reality beyond that of the material world. This was the knowledge possessed and disseminated by the 'real poets' but which had been lost or, as in her own case, actively forgotten by a culture that had given itself over to a 'materialist philosophy' that 'precludes orders of reality and value other than the physical'.[32] What had taken place through the rise of Scientism was a revolution that had 'reversed the normal hierarchy of values'.[33] What was on bottom of the ancient Great Chain of Being – matter – was now on top, and 'truth' meant the kind of attention to quantifiable detail to the exclusion of all else – the new way of knowing – that Goethe had warned would lead to a spiritually vacuous world. 'Truth' now in the arts meant 'true to life', which for Raine and her sympathetic contemporaries meant 'true to the lowest expression of the lowest intelligence', the kitchen sinks and unmade and often soiled beds of 'realism'.[34]

Art in her time – and in ours – was 'in your face', confronting its audience with the sordid banalities from which, as Raine noted, it had once released them. What use is such an art to the soul, she asked, which has no need to be reminded of 'life' – which, in any case, is unavoidable – but which desires and needs reminders of 'an order of perfection with which the common world is out of tune'?[35] Decades before its popularity, Raine predicted the rise of 'reality TV', pointing out that what is on the screen is often no different from the lives of those watching it. 'Viewers and viewed', she observed, 'could change places and nothing would be altered'.[36] If a work of imagination had once been a 'magic glass in which we discover that nature to which actuality is barely an approximation', it had become in our time a kind of brightly lit bathroom mirror, in which all the blemishes and wrinkles of 'real life' were magnified a hundredfold.[37] It seemed that not only had we lost beauty, we ignored it or even actively defaced it. Raine believed that at least some of this reaction grew from a resentment against the high standard that beauty set. It was, as Rilke said, the beginning of a terror that we are just able to bear, and dismissing it entirely was more bearable than admitting that one could not live up to its demands.

There was, she knew, a truth, a reality that was different from 'realism'. This was the reality of what she came to call Tradition and which was rooted in the teachings of Plato, Plotinus, the *Hermetica* and other forms of what has been called the 'perennial philosophy'.[38] This placed spirit or mind or imagination in the driver's seat, with the material world as a necessary but subordinate adjunct, occupying the bottom rung of the ontological ladder. It was to this Tradition that Henry Corbin alluded when he spoke of the imagination's need for 'access to a cosmology structured similarly to that of the traditional oriental philosophies, with a plurality of universes arranged in ascending order,' to keep it from losing itself in the will-to-power and its horrible productions.[39]

Such a cosmology seems light years away from a culture that embraces Big Bangs and the meaningless universes they create, which sees human beings as, at best, merely a higher form of animal (and applauds every expression of the animal in us) and at worst a stimulus-response machine, pushed and pulled by the ineluctable forces of cause-and-effect, whether on the mechanical, genetic or atomic level. Yet as Raine reminds us – and remembering is essential here – this access lies within us and is there, ever ready for our call. As Plato, from whom much of this Tradition emerges, knew, we possess a 'latent knowledge' of an order inherent within reality and within our soul. This is the harmony that Pythagoras had taught and lived long ago and which informed one of the 'two permanent needs of human nature' that Francis Cornford had recognised.

We perceive beauty, the Neo-Platonic philosopher Plotinus said, when we perceive something that is in accord with our soul. Beauty is a possession of our soul and we possess it most intensely when we are true to our being. This was something Raine found when she ignored the needs of her soul so as to fit in to the intellectual atmosphere of Cambridge. There was no beauty in that world, not only because it modelled itself on the requirements of positivism, but also because there was nothing in it that resonated with her soul. Knowledge of beauty is knowledge of soul. It is self-knowledge, and when we discover beauty we are discovering part of ourselves. This was, as Goethe knew, the harmony of the hidden law in the world with the hidden law within ourselves.

Unlike the rules of prosody that the scientific criticism she had learned required her to apply in order to analyse the formal structure of a poem, beauty to Raine and to all others sensitive to it, appeared all at once. Knowledge and the experience of beauty were one. We can learn of beauty only from beauty; no amount of theory can lead us to it, just as the most meticulously quantified description of a flower remains categorically less than the act of seeing one. Like Ernst Jünger's 'master key', the recognition of beauty is 'immediate and intuitive' and is achieved through a faculty 'higher than discursive reason'.[40] This is the Platonic *nous,* the Mind higher than reason that is dormant within us but which will respond to reflections of itself in the forms of the beautiful.

These are many. Unlike the 'blank slate' psychology which tells us that our soul is nothing more than a reflection of the outer world, beauty tells us that the soul contains a 'plenitude of forms', is indeed those forms itself, seeing itself in Nature's glass. (*Contra* Locke, nature is a reflection of the soul, not the other way around.) While 'realism' in its many forms strives to depict the material facts of things, including nature, true art reaches to the true nature, the archetype, by finding it and its reflection in natural things. Hence Plato and Plotinus' caution that to copy from nature is to copy from a copy. The true artist is 'original', not by being shockingly novel, but by reaching to the 'origin', the *Urphänomen,* from which all 'copies' arise. It is to awaken our recollection of these that poetry and the other arts exist. They hold before us images that tell us of our lost home. And we know we are recalling it. The assurance of this is the haunting sense of the *familiar* that overcomes us in its presence. True beauty is nothing strange or alien but achingly familiar, like the taste of Proust's *madeleine,* which reminds us of what we already know but have forgotten. All knowledge, Plato tells us, is such remembrance.

The knowledge we receive in this way is not of fact but of quality, of value and meaning. As Owen Barfield knew, 'true poetry', Raine tells us, 'has the power of transforming consciousness'.[41] We perceive beauty, are open to its presence, through a change in the quality of our consciousness. Only like can know like. We must have beauty within ourselves to see it in the world. The mind that denies the reality of the soul denies the reality of beauty and will never see it, although at times the nostalgia for a place we have never been can seep through even the most stalwart reductionist defences. But this place we have never been is with us all the time. It is the true imagination, the inner firmament beyond Mount Qâf, that Paracelsus, Barfield, Goethe, Corbin, Suhrawardi and others we have looked at knew well and voyaged in.

The knowledge Raine spoke of and sought in her 'real poets' formed what she called 'the learning of the imagination', a teaching that was not about the imagination but was the imagination itself. Its curriculum was made up of the symbols, metaphors and images that informed her favourite poetry – with Owen Barfield she shared a love of the Romantics – and which constituted much of the 'hollowed out' iconography that the modern soul misunderstood and often did its best to undermine. 'Tradition,' she wrote in her major work on Blake, 'is the record of imaginative experience'. 'Traditional metaphysics' – that of Pythagoras, Plato and Plotinus – 'is neither vague, personal or arbitrary', as the learned dons at Cambridge had tried to convince her it was. 'It is the recorded history of imaginative thought and has … an accompanying language of symbol and myth'.[42] This is Henry Corbin's *mundus imaginalis,* 'a very precise order of reality, which corresponds to a precise mode of perception': the true imagination.

She had grown up with this knowledge and then had worked hard to lose it. But it came back to her through another real poet who was not then the thing. W.B. Yeats had, she knew, been a Theosophist and had practised magic in the Hermetic Order of the Golden Dawn. He had studied Swedenborg and Kabbalah and spoken with the spirits. Such things had worked against Yeats in the reigning positivist climate. Yeats knew the truth of Shelley's definition of poetry as the 'language of the imagination', a language 'not of definitions which measure, but of images which evoke knowledge'.[43] In his essay 'The Trembling of the Veil', Yeats tells of his experience with the magician Samuel MacGregor Mathers, then head of the Golden Dawn. Part of the Golden Dawn teaching was the training of the imagination, or of visualisation, to be more exact.[44] This entailed the use of Hindu *tattwa* symbols, representing the five elements: fire, water, air, earth and spirit. Mathers handed Yeats a card with a symbol on it and told him to press it to his forehead. When Yeats did, images appropriate for the symbol came to him involuntarily. A red triangle symbolising fire evoked the image of a black giant rising up out of desert ruins; this was of the order of the salamanders, Mathers said, and absolutely correct. Yeats rejected the idea that telepathy might be responsible when he later handed someone a card by mistake but they nevertheless saw images appropriate to it, and not to the card they thought it was. Inspired by this experience Yeats anticipated Jung's notion of a 'collective unconscious' when he wrote of his belief that 'images well up before the mind's eye from a deeper source than conscious or subconscious memory'.

Yeats affirmed his belief in a Platonic order of things in his poem 'Sailing to Byzantium', which presents the ancient Oriental city (the direction of light in Suhrawardi's gnostic Platonism) as a symbol of the *mundus imaginalis,* an archetypal capital of the 'human kingdom of the imagination', a hub of the interworld where the incarnate and discarnate, conscious and unconscious self, meet.[45] Rejecting the world in which whatever is 'begotten, born, and dies' loses itself in 'sensual neglect', the poet turns instead to 'monuments of unageing intellect'. He abjures his 'dying animal', his body, the 'portable tomb' of the Hermetists, and reaches for the 'artifice of eternity': timeless beauty.[46]

Other Platonic themes abound in Yeats. Like the 'gyres' that widen and widen, separating falcon and falconer in 'The Second Coming', and which represent the myth of the Platonic year, the cycle of ages from that of gold to iron, the *Kali yuga* in Hindu thought, which Yeats and Raine felt was upon us.[47] These vortices of time also inform Yeats' undeservedly neglected attempt at a modern symbolic knowledge system, *A Vision,* a work of 'lunar knowledge' that should be better known.[48]

Yeats learned much from the 'real poet' whose artifices of eternity provided Raine with a lifetime's work. Imagination was all for William Blake. 'The world of Imagination,' Blake wrote in *A Vision of the Last Judgement,* 'is the world of Eternity: it is the divine bosom into which we shall all go after the death of the Vegetated body'. It is an Infinite and Eternal world, where 'exist the Permanent Realities of Every Thing which we see reflected in the Vegetable Glass of Nature'. As Goethe did, Blake saw the Permanent Realities, the *Urphänomena,* and not only the physical shell. Imagination is the 'true man', the 'Divine Humanity', what

Blake calls 'Jesus, the Imagination'. It is the source of everything around us; 'All Things Exist in the Human Imagination,' Blake tells us, echoing the ancient Hermetic philosophy which teaches that 'within God' – *Nous* – 'everything lies in imagination'. As Blake wrote in *Jerusalem:* 'In your Bosom you bear your Heaven and Earth & all you behold; tho' it appears Without, it is Within, in your Imagination...'

This ability to feel the world within oneself – the ultimate destination of Suhrawardi's inner journeys – is felt by all 'real poets'. Keats, a less austere poet than either Yeats or Blake, knew it. He knew nature 'imaginatively' in a way in which it was not merely 'cognised but experienced; not observed, but lived'. 'If a sparrow come before my window I take part in its existence and pick about the gravel', said the poet for whom truth was beauty and beauty truth.[49]

Blake too knew that we become what we behold, that we, as Barfield would say, participate in it. Men had fallen asleep, into what he called the 'land of Ulro', when they became 'passive before a mechanised nature', as his student Yeats knew. This was the result of Urizen's – the intellect's – usurpation of power from Los, the imagination. But Nature itself is the imagination, when seen correctly, and it is men's thoughts that create the 'Satanic mills', 'charted streets', and 'mind-forged manacles' that, to mix up our poets, make this earth a 'dim, vast vale of tears' (Shelley). 'Birth, and copulation, and death' was how Eliot summed up our existence here, but Blake denied this. He knew, as did Henry Corbin, that 'the imagination is a purely spiritual faculty, independent of the physical organism and therefore able to continue to exist after the latter has disappeared'.[50] The sensible world, for Blake, was really a 'system of appearances ... inseparable from the mind or consciousness' that perceives them, and in so perceiving also, as Husserl knew, 'creates what it perceives'.[51]

As Raine has pointed out, Blake imbibed much of his philosophy from Swedenborg, although in his *Marriage of Heaven and Hell* he had some hard words to say about his master. Raine has dispelled the picture of Blake as an untutored mad genius, spewing out incoherent mythologies like a geyser from Jung's collective unconscious. Blake knew the Tradition, he was versed in the 'learning of the imagination', reading the *Hermetica,* Boehme, the alchemists and others. But along with uncovering the Blake of Tradition, Raine also rescued from obscurity one of his Platonic tutors.

Thomas Taylor was saved from the dreary life of a bank clerk when he was asked to give a series of lectures on one of his favourite authors, Plato, to gatherings held at the home of Blake's friend and much more successful fellow artist, John Flaxman. Flaxman's invitation changed Taylor's life. Many of London's intelligentsia attended his lectures – Blake among them – and with their help Flaxman was able to secure a position for Taylor with the Society for the Encouragement of the Arts (later the Royal Society of the Arts). So began the career of 'the English Pagan', Thomas Taylor, the Platonist.

Taylor was born in London to a Dissenting family in 1758. Most likely he would have become a minister like his father, but an unacceptable marriage cast Taylor out of the family fold and into the cold world. A love of numbers and mathematics – more Pythagorean than commercial – secured him a place as a bank clerk. Most of his life was lived in poverty. His health was never very good, and his quiet, unworldly character must have given the impression that he was not long for this world. He did have some ambitions, though. As a young man he contrived an invention he called the 'perpetual light' – an apt name, given his philosophical predilections – that used phosphorus. Taylor may have thought that this eternal flame would bring him riches. Sadly, when he demonstrated it one evening at London's Freemason's Hall, it blew up and almost caused a fire.

Taylor had better luck with languages. He had a formidable memory and it informed his peculiar talent for ancient Greek and Latin. He was said to have conversed with his wife only in Greek; one assumes she knew it too, otherwise it would have been a rather one-sided conversation. He discovered Plato in his early twenties and was immediately captured by the great philosopher. A reading of the Neoplatonist Proclus triggered a kind of mystical experience. Like the philosophers he was reading, Taylor believed that we can know the divine only by becoming divine ourselves; his reading of Proclus accomplished this for him. The outcome was what he described as a 'perpetual serenity, unceasing delight, and occasional rapture'.[52]

Taylor's illumination led to a prodigious output. He produced the first English translations of the complete works of Plato and Aristotle, and made many translations of Plotinus, Proclus and the 'divine Iamblichus'. Taylor also wrote extensively on the Orphic tradition and the influence Orphic mythology had on the Neoplatonists. The late eighteenth century was not the best time, however, for Taylor's inspired translations to appear. Mechanistic science was on the rise and the quantitative mindset looked askance at what it saw as a muddle of woolly-minded mystifications. Taylor's work was ignored or, at best, severely criticised by the literary mainstream, but his real readers were more open-minded than this, and recognised in his writings a unique offering.[53] They knew, Raine tells us, that Taylor lay before them 'a great field of excluded knowledge which the schools, dominated by the materialist climate of the time, do not recognise'.[54]

Blake read and learned from Taylor, but he was not alone. Later poets like Shelley and Keats read him; Yeats too. Ralph Waldo Emerson ranked Taylor as one of the 'Immortals' in his book *Representative Men* – Plato, Goethe and Swedenborg were included as well – and claimed that he was 'a better man of imagination, a better poet, than any English writer between Milton and Wordsworth'. Other important figures in the 'learning of the imagination' who appreciated Taylor's work were Madame Blavatsky, co-founder of the Theosophical Society; her secretary, the Gnostic and Hermetic scholar G.R.S. Mead; and the esoteric encyclopaedist Manly P. Hall.

To his audience at John Flaxman's home Taylor spoke of Orpheus, Hermes, Zoroaster and the 'perennial philosophy', the 'primal wisdom' of the ancients which Plato had imbibed from the sages who preceded him. Taylor was a one-man Platonic Academy, doing for the esoteric intelligentsia of late eighteenth century London what Marsilio Ficino did for the artists and poets of Renaissance Florence, with his Latin translations of the lost books of Plato and the *Hermetica*.[55] Taylor believed that this primal wisdom was 'coeval with the universe itself; and however its continuity may be broken by opposing systems, it will make its appearance at different periods of time, as long as the sun himself shall continue to illumine the world'.[56]

One important efflorescence of this perennial philosophy

appeared, Raine argued, in English Romantic poetry, whose symbols, imagery and aims, she maintained, are practically identical with Neoplatonism. Through Taylor, Blake learned of the ancient wisdom, absorbing the insight that the sages wrote obscurely, in mysterious images and arcane myths that needed to be read symbolically in order to pass beyond their surface, literal meaning. Blake even suffered to learn of mathematics from Taylor, but was too impatient a poet to do this for long. *Contra* Plato, he concluded that God was more an artist than a geometer. As Raine makes clear in her essays on Blake and Yeats, Blake was more of a prophetic poet than a Platonic one, and while Yeats turned his eye and hand to perfection of form – Platonic beauty – Blake was more like a seer of old, driven by a holy energy and demonic life.

Another poet also touched by Taylor's inspiration had a more philosophical bent. In his classic 'study in the ways of the imagination', *The Road to Xanadu,* John Livingstone Lowes points out that Taylor was one of Samuel Taylor Coleridge's 'darling studies'.[57] Coleridge studied Taylor's translations deeply and, with much else, they fired his imagination, providing many of the ingredients that went into 'The Rime of the Ancient Mariner' and that most imaginative poem about the imagination, 'Kubla Khan'. In a kind of 'wish list' that Coleridge gave to a friend shortly before writing the poem – which came to Coleridge in an opium-induced hypnagogic trance, only to be truncated by a visitor from Porlock – the poet asked for copies of Taylor's renditions of Iamblichus, Proclus and Porphyry, as well as some titles by Ficino.[58] According to Raine, the perennial philosophy acted as a kind of thread, linking together with its perpetual theme the many and varied images and metaphors that came together in Coleridge's haunting poem. 'In the literature of Tradition – the learning of the imagination,' she writes, 'Coleridge was deeply versed'.[59]

Coleridge's caves of ice, sunless seas and caverns measureless to man where 'Alph, the sacred river ran' are, Raine argues, all in 'strict accordance' with the 'symbolic vocabulary of Neoplatonism', and evoke in the sensitive reader that strange nostalgia and familiarity with a place where we have never been but know painfully well.[60] The poem 'both is, and is about, remembrance'. Its theme, she writes, 'is the imaginative experience itself', and is 'written in that exaltation of wonder which invariably accompanies moments of insight into the mystery upon whose surface we live'.[61] As Plato said long ago, and as his readers Raine and Barfield knew, poetry is itself a transformation of consciousness, both for the poet writing it and for its proper readers.

Coleridge was a 'library cormorant', reading perpetually in what he called 'out of the way books'. Along with Taylor's Neoplatonist works he was also familiar with what was coming out of Germany, with Kant, Schelling and *Naturphilosophie.* Coleridge shared much with Goethe, but where Goethe kept his focus firmly on sensuous phenomena and claimed never to have thought about thinking – something he scolded his fellow Germans for constantly doing – Coleridge at times seems as if he did little else. In many ways he should be considered England's home-grown metaphysician, in the classic German manner. And yet the comparison with Goethe remains. Where Goethe worked to achieve 'active seeing', Coleridge worked to do the same, but with thinking. Both saw the process under their observation – or rather, with which they participated – as essentially creative, in the way with which many of the people we have looked at would have agreed.

In Chapter XIII of his *Biographia Literaria,* Coleridge made his famous distinctions between the Primary Imagination, Secondary Imagination and Fancy. Primary Imagination, he said, is 'the living power and prime agent of all human perception', something with which Blake would surely have agreed. It is 'a repetition in the finite mind of the eternal act of creation in the infinite I AM'. When we perceive the world then, according to Coleridge, we echo the Creator's creation of it. Our perception is itself creative, something Husserl knew.

Secondary imagination, that of the artist, poet and creative thinker is an 'echo' of the Primary Imagination, 'co-existing with the conscious will', and differing from the Primary Imagination only by degree. It 'dissolves, diffuses, and dissipates, in order to recreate'. Its action is always and essentially vital, that is living, having an 'inside', whereas objects, as objects, are fixed and dead. In this it is identical to Corbin's practice of *ta'wil,* which saves phenomena from objectification and idolatry, by returning them to the archetype, or Goethe's 'active seeing'. Fancy, as we've seen, has only these 'fixities' to play with and is 'nothing more than a mode of memory emancipated from the order of time and space'. It is not creative as the secondary imagination is.[62]

This creative character of the imagination Coleridge called the 'esemplastic power'. Esemplastic is a coinage of Coleridge's, and is itself an example of the very process it defines. It means to 'shape into one', to take disparate things and through an act of creative imagination, unify them into a whole. Coleridge had come across a similar term in Schelling, *Ineinsbildung* – literally 'in-one-shaping' – which meant an 'interweaving of opposites' and he sought to find an equivalent in English. There was none, so he invented one, taking his cue from the Greek. It is this 'shaping power' of the imagination that differentiates it from fancy. The result of using the esemplastic power, which Coleridge argues is a distinct action of the mind – indeed, its fundamental action – is a new perception, arising out of the creative unity of different elements. For all its interest in 'novelty', fancy can only return to the same old things. It is imagination which is truly 'original', because it returns to the origin of all things, itself.

The idea of a creative unity transcending the opposites from which it arises is at the heart of Coleridge's insights into polarity, something again which he shared with Goethe. Coleridge claimed that if he were granted 'a nature having two contrary forces, the one of which tends to expand infinitely, while the other strives to apprehend or to find itself in this infinity,' he could cause 'the world of intelligences with the whole system of their representations' to rise up before us.[63] Coleridge's two forces are Goethe's 'systole' and 'diastole' and Schelling's 'expansion' and 'contraction'. They form the centre of what Owen Barfield, who wrote a book devoted exclusively to what Coleridge thought, called 'polar logic'.

Polar logic is behind Blake's 'proverbs of hell' that 'Opposition is True Friendship' and 'Without Contraries there is no Progress'. Polar logic is not the same as having logical opposites. These are merely contradictory and only cancel each other out. Polar opposites exist, Barfield says, 'by virtue of each other, and are generative of new products'.[64] They are opposites as are day and night, but they need each other to exist. They are radically different, but inseparable and are in a dynamic, not static, relationship. It is the tension between them that provides the energy for creative transformation. Polarity, as Barfield says, is 'the manifestation of one power by opposite forces'.[65]

Barfield admits that this may not be immediately understandable. In fact he would even say that to try to understand it, in Coleridge's use of the term 'understand', would defeat the purpose. Defining polarity in Coleridge's sense is as difficult and ultimately self-defeating as trying to define imagination itself – or life or existence, for that matter – in explicit, 'factual' terms. Barfield asks: 'how much use are definitions of the undefinable?' Polarity must be grasped by the imagination 'in a glance' in order for us to recognise it and its importance. In this it has much in common with the *symbolique* of Schwaller de Lubicz, the ability to perceive contradictory meanings in the same object. Echoing Coleridge, Barfield even says that recognising polarity is itself 'the basic act of imagination'. In other words, one grasps polarity by experiencing it, just as one must experience imagination, or beauty, in order to know it.

The fundamental polarity of our experience, Coleridge saw, is that of the self and the world, the inner and the outer. He saw the mind as a kind of 'current', like electricity, running between the two.[66] According to Barfield, Coleridge argues that it is the task of the imagination to help us experience this polarity, this current, immediately and intensely. As it is now, we don't – or at least this is true of most of us. We perceive the outer world but are unaware of our contribution to our experience of it; that is, we are unaware of our mind's, through the Primary Imagination, participation in 'the world'. We experience only one pole. Just as we are unaware of our perception as active, as 'intentional', in Husserl's term, we are unaware of the activity of our minds. We are aware of our thoughts, but not, Coleridge argues, of our thinking. We lack what he called 'the mind's self-experience in the act of thinking'.

Using the medieval terms, we are aware of *Natura naturata,* that is 'nature' as a passive finished product (our thoughts), but not *Natura naturans,* nature as the active cause of itself (our thinking). By thinking here Coleridge does not mean the content of our thoughts, what we are 'thinking about', but the live character of thought itself. We accept our thoughts and our thinking passively.

Coleridge believed it was vital that we become aware of the act of thinking itself. Imagination, he saw, was the way to do this.

Imagination can do this because it in itself is 'precisely an advance of the mind towards knowing itself in the object'.[67] Without imagination, we do not know ourselves in the objects we perceive. We are aware of only one side of our polar relationship, that of the 'objectified' world. This is 'objectified', 'fixed and dead', precisely because we do not perceive it with imagination, but only with what Coleridge calls 'understanding'.

Understanding, in Coleridge's use, is essentially the 'new way' of knowing we have discussed throughout this book. It posits a completely separate 'world' 'outside' consciousness which it thinks 'about' in terms of conventional logic, and sees ourselves as separate and distinct bodies within this world. Understanding can analyse and manipulate the 'objects' in this world, and in that sense is active. But it is passive regarding itself. As it sees only an objectified, non-living world – because it perceives it without imagination – it, as Yeats said, becomes hypnotised before a 'mechanised nature'. It becomes what it beholds.

We can free ourselves from what is 'essentially a sleeping relationship with phenomena' and enter into a 'waking one', Coleridge tells us, by becoming aware of the other pole of experience, that is, our own minds.[68] Until we do, we are subject to what Coleridge calls 'the lethargy of custom'.[69] This is our habit of seeing the world around us as 'everyday' and 'ordinary', of looking at it from the 'natural standpoint' and taking it for granted. Through the lethargy of custom we grow used to everything. It becomes 'uninteresting'. We become apathetic and to relieve our *ennui* we relinquish our active imagination entirely and give ourselves up to 'entertainments' devised to divert us from boredom, which, of course, only weakens our imagination more.[70]

We can escape this sleep through an activity Barfield calls 'completing'.[71] Completing 'unites clearness with depth' – rather like Jünger's 'stereoscopy' – and 'the plenitude of the senses with the comprehensibility of the understanding'. It accomplishes this through the imagination, which impregnates the understanding with itself, thus transforming its mere surface awareness to an 'intuitive and a living power'.[72] In doing this, understanding is transformed into what Coleridge calls 'reason', which is an 'organ of spiritual apprehension'.[73] Such apprehension has 'objects consubstantial' with itself for its perception.[74] That is, it is itself its own object. It is self-contemplative.[75] By knowing the world through imagination, it knows itself. And while this 'spiritual reason' cannot be understood by its less imaginative cousin, it can, like the images that arose in Yeats' mind, be evoked and expressed in symbols, which are themselves products of this reason and a means of triggering the imaginative power necessary to experience them.

Coleridge understood – in his imaginative sense – that the relations between the elements of a polarity are dynamic. That is, they are in motion and changing. One pole cannot be without the other – this is why a term like 'bipolar' is redundant, as you cannot have one pole: if you had only one, it would not be a pole. But Coleridge knew that it is the nature of a polar relationship that one pole can dominate for a time, and that the shifts in dominances between the poles are the motor of all life and evolution, the 'contraries' that produce 'progress'.

But what happens when one pole dominates for too long, so that the polarity loses its active, creative character and takes on a more hierarchical one, with one pole on top? What happens when only one of the 'two permanent needs of human nature' is satisfied, while the other is ignored and left to languish, or to meet its needs as best it can? How is the imbalance corrected? And how is imagination involved?

This seems to be where we walked in.

Chapter Six
The Responsible Imagination

I began this book by saying that a new way of knowing the world and ourselves arose in the early seventeenth century and quickly came to occupy a position of importance and authority that now, some four centuries later, seems unshakeable. To be sure, many have questioned its authority and accuracy in dealing with aspects of our experience that it seems ill-equipped to address. We have seen that even at the outset of this new way of knowing, the 'spirit of geometry' was advised not to forget its close cousin the 'spirit of finesse' and that it should not dismiss its contribution to our understanding of ourselves and the world. The person who raised this concern, Blaise Pascal, had the credentials to do so. He was both a mathematician and logician and a soul sensitive to the deeper, more ambiguous significances of human existence. He could ponder the complexities of number theory and work out the intricacies of what later became probability theory, essential to our modern use of statistics, but he was also concerned with the meaning of human life and the ever-present imponderables that make it a mystery.

Many came after Pascal and one could write a history of modern Western consciousness from the point of view of the scores of important figures that have echoed his concern. A list would include Nobel Prize winners, celebrated writers, artists, poets and philosophers. By now it would include filmmakers.[1] To tally it up would be tedious, but it could be done, and most readers I suspect could reel off a handful of names if pressed. Even as towering a figure as Einstein comes down on the side of the 'other' way of knowing. In an interview in 1929 with *The Saturday Evening Post,* Einstein said: 'I believe in intuitions and inspirations. I sometimes feel that I am right. I do not know that I am'. He said that when expeditions, financed by the Royal Academy, were sent out to South America and Africa to confirm his theory of relativity – which they did during the solar eclipse of 29 May, 1919 – he was not surprised when he was proved right. 'I would have been surprised,' he said, 'if I had been proved wrong'.[2] When the journalist George Sylvester Viereck asked Einstein if he trusted his imagination more than his knowledge, Einstein replied: 'Imagination is more important than knowledge. Knowledge is limited. Imagination encircles the world'.[3]

Not long after this interview, Einstein repeated this remark in his book *Cosmic Religion* which appeared in 1931 with a preface by the playwright Bernard Shaw. At the time Shaw, like Einstein, was one of the most famous men in the world. Shaw was a great prophet of the imagination, seeing it as the driving force behind what, following the philosopher Henri Bergson, he called 'creative evolution', as opposed to Darwin's more mechanical variety. In *Back to Methuselah* (1922), Shaw's anti-Darwinian 'Metabiological Pentateuch', Shaw argued that a persistent enough will informed by a powerful enough imagination and focused on purposes beyond its own – that is, on wider, impersonal values – could defeat even death, or at least keep it at bay long enough to increase the human life span considerably. Shaw believed we needed this extra time in order to mature as full human beings and he himself lived to the age of ninety-six. 'Imagination,' Shaw wrote, 'is the beginning of creation. You imagine what you desire; you will what you imagine; and at last you create what you will'.[4]

Einstein was not so forceful a prophet, but his belief in imagination as a creative power was no less than Shaw's. In *Cosmic Religion* he wrote that: 'Imagination embraces the entire world, stimulating progress, giving birth to evolution. It is, strictly speaking, a real factor in scientific research'. Einstein showed that he too had a copy of Ernst Jünger's 'master key' when he remarked that: 'At times I feel certain I am right without knowing the reason'.[5]

As we seen, those who follow the spirit of finesse – as Einstein is doing here – find it difficult, if not impossible, to explain how they know what they know. They cannot express it directly and can at best speak only in metaphor, analogy, or symbol. Einstein knew, but he didn't know how he knew, or at least he wasn't able to say how he knew, in the kind of language scientists are supposed to use when they talk about their discoveries. They are supposed to carefully lay out all the details for everyone to see, and if required, walk us through the steps. Einstein knew in the way that scientists are not supposed to know. He knew in our 'other' way of knowing.

Yet even with endorsements from Einstein, a Nobel Prize winner – Shaw was one too – imagination still takes a backseat to the more wieldy kind of knowing that we feel we are more familiar with. We think we are more familiar with this kind of knowledge but in a sense that is not really true. We know the other way of knowing just as well and we use it all the time, often more than we do our 'official' means of knowledge. But we don't see it as a way of knowing. We say it is 'just imagination' because we have been taught to do so. If we are more familiar with the quantitative way of knowing, that is because we are taught that this is knowing, and that anything else is wishful thinking and make believe.

This has left us in the position that I described at the end of the last chapter, with one side of a polarity dominating too much for too long. The quantitative way of knowing, that treats the world as objective, neutral and absolutely independent of our consciousness, seems to have gained an ascendancy that threatens to completely eclipse its necessary but marginalised more participatory other half. The opposition that is true friendship has broken down, and the contraries are not progressing. They are stuck in a fruitless contradiction and have been so for some time. But the situation is even worse than this. One pole virtually denies the reality of the other. And if the concerns of people like Iain McGilchrist are valid, this does not bode well for the future. It may be the case that, as McGilchrist warns, what we have in store for us is a kind of 'twenty-first century schizoid man', in the words of an old song.[6]

Proponents of the other way of knowing have been aware of this imbalance and as we've seen, many of them have tried in different ways to rectify it. Goethe tried to harmonise his science and his poetry. Suhrawardi directed his efforts toward those 'who aspire at once to both mystical experience and philosophical knowledge', to intuition and logic, a goal that his modern interpreter, Henry Corbin, also pursued. Ernst Jünger sought to see things 'in stereo', as it were, perceiving their surface and their depths simultaneously.

Kathleen Raine found the same beauty that haunted her in Romantic poetry within her studies of botany and zoology. Pascal knew both the 'spirit of geometry' and the 'spirit of finesse'. Jacques Barzun maintains that anyone can be taught to think like Euclid and Walt Whitman.

It seems there is no inherent barrier to both sides of our cognitive polarity working together creatively. It may not be easy to do. But it is possible. Given this, what should be our next course of action?

If it is the case that we are favouring our critical, analytical mind at the expense of our creative, imaginative one, then clearly it would seem that what we need to do is to cut back on analysis and increase our imagination. That in fact is what the students of the 'learning of the imagination' we have been looking at did. But even here there are problems and concerns. Imagination alone, it seems, is not enough. Or to put it another way: will any imagination do, or are there limits and guidelines that imagination should follow in order to bring a creative balance back into the polarity between our two ways of knowing?

We've seen that Henry Corbin saw the need for a tradition to keep the imagination from spilling over into 'reckless wastefulness'. Without such a tradition Corbin believed that the imagination could, in partnership with our 'will-to-power', become a 'never-ending source of horrors'. Goethe was careful to ground his Primal Plant in what he saw as its 'inner necessity and truth'. Otherwise it would have been merely an example of 'the shadowy phantoms of vain imagination'. Paracelsus counselled that we need to stay close to the *imaginatio vera,* otherwise we would embrace the 'madman's cornerstone' and find ourselves engaged in an 'exercise of thought without foundation in nature'. Coleridge recognised the essential difference between an imagination infused into the understanding, which produces the 'reason' that enables us to grasp the living reality of experience, and the 'flights of fancy' that propel themselves by welding together the fragments of images and ideas inhabiting our minds into some 'novel' arrangement which may amuse us for a moment but which lacks all true life.

It seems imagination alone is not enough. It must be guided by limits and criteria that in some way match the concerns of the students of the imagination mentioned previously. The idea is not for imagination to take the place of the analytical, quantitative mind, just as the analytical, quantitative mind should not have pushed its intuitive partner out of the picture four centuries ago. The idea is for them to work together, or at least to recognise the need for each other, to see in each other one of our 'two permanent needs of human nature' and to work to accommodate both. Satisfying one need at the expense of the other does not work, whichever need is in question. Starving the analytical mind would be as much a mistake as the present marginalising of our intuitive consciousness is. Indeed, we can account for the aggressive campaign against the intuitive kind of knowledge that was waged in the early seventeenth century at least in part by looking at the damper the Church had held down on free intellectual inquiry prior to this.[7] Let loose, the spirit of inquiry would not suffer restraint and so it worked to ensure it would not be inhibited again. Hence the 'meaningless' universe we now inhabit, necessarily so, as 'meaning' is amenable to the intuitive mind, not the analytical one. The analytical, quantitative mind has freed itself of the constraints of religion or any other belief that would check its untrammelled growth. A by-product of that liberation is the sense of pointlessness that permeates our early twenty-first century consciousness. Had the new way of knowing not had to do battle against such opposition – and had the Church not paradoxically joined forces with it briefly, in order to eliminate their mutual rival, the Hermetic sciences – then it is possible that the kind of knowledge Goethe believed was good for us may have been the outcome, and not, as seems to be the case, the kind that he believed was pernicious.[8]

Unfortunately, the creative polarity that is possible but not guaranteed in the individual is even less easy to achieve in a whole culture, which is, of course, made up of individuals. With some important exceptions, that nevertheless show such a harmony can be achieved, what tends to happen is a kind of pendulum swing from one side to the other, with a build-up of reason and rationality triggering a plunge into the dark waters of the unconscious, and a desire for clarity and light then leading to a denial of those waters' existence. One such swing happened with Romanticism which gave way to Symbolism, then Dada, Surrealism, and the absurd. Another happened in the 1960s, with the 'occult revival' that took place in that decade leading to the 'counter-culture' and eventually the 'New Age' that has been with us now for some time.[9] Both reacted to an excess of the quantitative mind-set; for Romanticism it was the Enlightenment and in the 1960s it was the buttoned-down 'atomic age' of the 1950s. And as these swings are neither precise nor controlled, in trying to compensate for the previous excess, they create excesses of their own. Getting it 'just right' as Goldilocks did, requires a kind of pinpoint accuracy – that 'master key' – when analysis and intuition, quantity and quality meet and produce something new, creative, vital, and which extends the borders of our consciousness and of our lives. That it can happen is, as we've seen, entirely possible. That it doesn't happen often enough is the unfortunate thing.

What can happen when imagination 'in the raw', without the kind of guidelines I've been speaking of, lets rip, and tries to compensate for the imbalance on its own? I think the kind of concerns raised by Erich Kahler, Jacques Barzun, William Barrett and Kathleen Raine, that I looked at in the previous chapter, can give us an idea. There is of course a long history of how art became associated with revolt, nihilism and the rejection of such 'bourgeois' ideas as beauty and harmony, and embraced wholeheartedly what we today call the 'transgressive'. I cannot go into that here and the reader can get a very good overview of this in Barzun's lectures *The Use and Abuse of Art* mentioned earlier. Barzun and the others raised their concerns half a century ago, and the reader may wonder if things are still quite so bad and if these worries aren't really out of date. I don't see that in the time that has passed much has changed. Artists today make fortunes displaying preserved sharks, unmade beds, or defaced walls.[10] And as Kathleen Raine predicted, the most popular television programmes today are some version of 'reality TV' in which millions of viewers watch people 'just like them' do all sorts of things, usually having to do with sex and humiliation.[11] There is much of the commonplace in all of this but not, I believe, much transfiguration.

Of course, according to the demotic tone of our times, beauty, or its lack, is in the eye of its beholder and no doubt many people find these developments exciting and important. But my own taste falls more on the side of 'monuments of unageing intellect' than on the evidence that proves Andy Warhol was right and that 'art is what you can get away with'.[12]

However, if overpriced and indecorous art is all we have to be concerned with, we could ignore what we don't like and look for what we do, though it seems less easy these days to find 'monuments of unageing intellect' or transfiguring beauty. What turns up in galleries and museums and generates enormous sums at auction is, as it were, only the early warning system for something that may have much wider consequences.[13]

Owen Barfield, we've seen, saw a need for a responsibility of the imagination. This grew out of the simple recognition that imagination can be either good or bad, to speak in the simplest terms. When the Romantics first rejected the constraints of Enlightenment rationality, they believed that an unrestricted imagination was in itself a good, just as the early rationalists held in check by the Church, believed that indiscriminate knowledge in itself was a good. By now we can see that the early restrictions on both sides have long been overcome and that each has been free for some time now to pursue their course. We have looked at some of the consequences of that in this book. Barfield's concern about being responsible for and to one's imagination was aroused by precisely the kind of art that Barzun, Kahler, Barrett and Raine remarked on. But it was not so much that he didn't like seeing 'pictures of a dog with six legs emerging from a vegetable marrow or a woman with a motorcycle substituted for her left breast' – he didn't in fact – as that he was concerned that such things would start to take over reality.[14] Just as the change in consciousness that he experienced when reading poetry required an effort of imagination on his part, an effort of will, so too the people who do like seeing such things will make such an effort to see them. Barfield was concerned that if enough people made that effort, or, through the 'lethargy of custom', let others make it for them and passively accepted the results, the world would eventually come to look like that. Barfield made these remarks in 1957, when *Saving the Appearances* was first published. I will leave it to the reader to judge whether in the sixty years that have passed anything like Barfield's concerns has happened.

Like everyone else in this book, Barfield took the creative power of imagination seriously. Paracelsus, we've seen, believed he could 'stab and wound' with a thought, and he took for granted that the mind could make the body ill. Blake and Coleridge have no doubt about the creative powers of imagination. For Blake, 'All Things Exist in the Human Imagination', and Coleridge agrees, seeing in Primary Imagination 'the living power and prime agent of all human perception'. In this it is second only to 'the eternal act of creation in the infinite I AM'. That is, the imagination behind our perceiving the world is the same as the imagination that creates it. Coleridge even says it is a 'repetition' of that act of creation. When we open our eyes and see the world we are at the same time in some way creating it, or at least are participating in our 'finite' way in its 'eternal' creation. Rudolf Steiner agreed with Coleridge. 'Man is not only there in order to form for himself a picture of the finished world,' he tells us. 'Nay, he himself cooperates in bringing the world into existence'. 'The content of reality,' Steiner assures us, 'is only the reflection of the content of our minds'.

We may think: Well, Steiner was a mystic, Blake and Coleridge were poets, Paracelsus was an alchemist. Weren't they letting their own imagination run away with them? But we've seen that science and philosophy agree with them. Ever since Werner Heisenberg we've known that the observer alters the observed, and Goethe knew this before Heisenberg. And Paul Ricoeur, a rigorous French philosopher awarded many academic honours with no interest in the occult, has argued that we can best understand Husserl (another difficult no-nonsense thinker) if we can grasp that 'the intentionality which culminates in seeing' – Husserl's 'perception is intentional' – is a kind of 'creative vision'. Each of these thinkers, and there are many others like them, believe that in a very real sense our imagination, our consciousness, is in some way creative, not only in art, poetry, music, but in reality itself. In some sense for them we do indeed 'create reality', or at least are an essential agent in its coming into being. Imagination then is not about 'make believe' but about 'make real'.

Our rejected occult or esoteric tradition has long recognised this. 'Don't call up what you can't put down' is solid magical advice, and the overconfident protagonists of many occult horror tales have learned it to their dismay.[15] Thoughts are things, very powerful ones, this tradition tells us, and it is prudent to be aware of their power. Goethe warned of the power of an ardent wish. 'Be careful what you wish for in youth,' he advised, because 'you will get it in middle age'. Yeats, we know, echoed him: 'Whatever we build in the imagination will accomplish itself in the circumstances of our lives'. The writer John Cowper Powys, whose mammoth *A Glastonbury Romance* is perhaps the most mystical novel in the English language, was so convinced of the power of his 'evil eye', his ability, like Paracelsus', of causing harm at a distance, that he took enormous, complicated precautions so that he would not, through some chance act of imagination and will, inadvertently harm those around him.[16]

According to the twentieth century's most famous magician, Aleister Crowley, 'Magick is the Science and Art of causing change to occur in conformity with Will'.[17] Crowley knew, as his contemporary Bernard Shaw did, that the will cannot work in a vacuum, and that before we can apply our will, we must have a clear idea of what we are willing. That is the business of the imagination. It is, as Shaw said, the beginning of creation. Barfield's concern is precisely this. He had no doubts that imagination is powerful, as is the will. The question is: what do you imagine? What do you will into creation? Desire, Shaw said, starts it off. We imagine what we desire and then will to make it real. Of course not every stray thought or fancy is creative. There are, it seems, some safeguards in place; we should be thankful for this, otherwise the world would be filled with the phantoms of our inconstant desire – although in many ways our multiple modes of technological self-entertainment approach precisely this arrangement. But the question remains: what do we want?

As evidence that his concern is warranted, Barfield points to what in effect was the 'creation' of Nature in the way we understand and experience it, by William Wordsworth and Coleridge with the publication of their *Lyrical Ballads* in 1798. Before the reader gasps 'What?' and points out that Nature existed well before Wordsworth and Coleridge, consider this. In 1773 Dr Samuel Johnson and his friend and biographer James Boswell, embarked on a tour of Scotland, much of which, at the time, was still wild and untamed.

Johnson's account of their travels, *A Journey to the Western Isles of Scotland* (1775), is peppered with complaints about the mountains and lakes his carriage had to go around. They made the journey tedious and long he said. Johnson liked his nature well ordered, in gardens with neat topiaries and much preferred the city. Today people spend great sums and make much effort precisely to get to the places Johnson wished he could have avoided. Wordsworth and Coleridge and the other Romantics taught their readers how to see Nature in a different way, as an object of beauty and a medium of what Wordsworth called 'unknown modes of being'.[18]

People of course knew Nature before, but the idea of the wilderness as something of value in itself, and not as a wasteland to be tamed, was new. Until then, Nature was a force to respect, and a resource to master and use. Humans for the most part were up against it in some way, struggling to eke out a life from it and to protect themselves from it. Now poets were singing of its power to soothe and heal and inspire the soul. We can say that the way to this new perception of Nature began in 1336 when the poet Petrarch climbed a mountain in southern France just to see the view, something, until then, that few people, if any, had thought of doing. Petrarch himself was considered mad for doing it.[19] But slowly the taste for it caught on. We can say that when Petrarch made his ascent of Mont Ventoux, he had started the nature tourist industry.

Four and a half centuries later, Wordsworth and Coleridge pressed the point home to their readers. By now it has reached many more people and has altered not only imaginations but also economies. As an example Barfield points out that 'the economic and social structure of Switzerland' which is determined in no small part by its tourist industry, has the Romantics to thank for the fact that 'the mountains that twentieth-century man sees are not the mountains that eighteenth-century man saw'.[20] The physical substance or 'matter' of the mountains is the same – although with the developments in elementary physics, perhaps we may not say even that – but the way it is 'represented' is different. Twentieth-century mountains are more symbolic than eighteenth-century ones because the Romantic movement taught us to see in mountains something more than merely their physical forms. They mean something more to us than they did to Dr Johnson, just as

Petrarch's mountain meant something more to him than it did to the people who tried to dissuade him from scaling its heights.

What turned non-symbolic mountains into symbolic ones? Imagination. And this has helped not only the Swiss. Nature reserves, national parks and wildlife preservation are direct outcomes of the alteration in our perception effected by what we can call the 'imagination explosion' that came with and produced the Romantics. I am not saying, nor is Barfield, that everyone who goes out into 'nature' today and seeks out the 'wild' as a source of beauty has read Wordsworth or even knows who he was. But I do think that the desire we have to do this is rooted in the change in our perception of Nature that the Romantics brought about.

What are mountains and the wilderness symbolic of? For the Romantics they meant a kind of freedom, an untamed, expansive, mysterious living world not reduced to the quantities and measurements of the new science. They felt this freedom in themselves, and the untamed world represented it for them. It was as if the vast outer spaces that had stunned Petrarch led to vast inner spaces being discovered within the human mind. Yet if these reflections on the impact of the imagination on reality seem too abstract, consider a more direct example of how the inner and outer worlds can permeate each other. Although it wasn't until late in his life that C.G. Jung spoke openly about the phenomenon he called 'synchronicity', he had in fact been preoccupied with it for decades. Synchronicity is Jung's coinage for what we can call 'meaningful coincidence', when the inner and outer worlds reflect each other with such accuracy and obvious meaning that to resort to mere coincidence as an explanation is useless. Jung tells the story of an extremely rationalist client of his, whose hyper-intellectualism made her difficult to treat. She was telling Jung about a dream involving a golden scarab when Jung heard a fluttering at the window. He opened it and a green-gold scarab flew in. That is a synchronicity. Jung's patient relented after that and her treatment progressed.

In 1951 Jung enlisted the aid of the physicist Wolfgang Pauli to try to account for the phenomenon of 'meaningful coincidence' by way of quantum physics. The result was their book *Synchronicity: An Acausal Connecting Principle.* Jung was trying to provide some scientific anchor for the experience, hence the term 'acausal connecting principle,' which, strictly speaking, means a causeless cause. Elements of a synchronicity are linked through meaning, not cause and effect, as they are in mechanical processes. The dream about the scarab and the actual scarab were in no way connected, at least in no usual way. But that the scarab should appear when Jung's client was recounting her dream seems to mean something. To Jung it meant that his client's inner world and her outer world were participating in each other. The impermeable barrier between them had been breached. The real scarab was telling her to take her dream scarab seriously. Or, rather than a barrier being breached, more likely the illusion that our inner and outer worlds are strictly separate had dissolved briefly, and the 'unconscious' – or whatever is responsible – had shown itself as an active agent in the so-called 'objective' world, and that it was taking a special interest in her case.

I am convinced that synchronicities are real, true phenomena, and in my book on Jung, I recount some examples of my own, as well as those of Jung.[21] I have no idea how they happen nor am I convinced by any attempt so far to explain them in terms of quantum physics, as Jung and Pauli tried to do. But I am as convinced of their reality as I am that of the desk I am sitting at and the computer I am writing on. In some ways I suspect that we will never explain them in any scientific way, except to say they seem to be an experience in which what is happening in our heads and what is happening in the outside world are directly related through meaning, and that some intelligence other than our own that knows more than we do is in some way behind them. They are, I believe, related to a condition of consciousness that at present we only experience intermittently but with which we will, with any luck, become more familiar.

But explaining synchronicities is not the point. I mention them as an example of how our inner world can affect the outer one. In some way that we cannot as yet understand, our inner world reaches out into the outer one, and arranges it so that a synchronicity will happen. I find they are almost always beneficial and seem to be a kind of nudge or gentle push to move in the right direction, or an acknowledgement that I am already doing so. And as seems to be the case, they tend to happen more when we are optimistic and positive minded.[22] And if optimism and a positive outlook can stimulate synchronicities, then it is clear that our minds can affect reality.

At this point, the notion that they can I think is more important to grasp than how they can. Perhaps the 'how' is only a mystery because we start from the position of the natural standpoint, that is, with the belief that the world is something 'out there' that our minds only reflect, and so there seems to be no way that they can in any way impress themselves upon it. As the 'blank slate' school of psychology tells us, the exact opposite is the truth: it impresses itself on us. But with this we are back where we began.

A.R. Orage, the literary critic and student of the esoteric teacher Gurdjieff, believed with Shaw that imagination is the propellant of evolution. 'Evolution is altogether an imaginative process,' he wrote. 'You become what you have been led to imagine yourself to be'.[23] Barfield would agree, but he would go one step further. Not only ourselves, but the world too, becomes what we imagine it to be. The phenomena which make up the 'world' are not independent of us. If as Blake tells us, we become what we behold, the opposite also holds true: what we behold becomes us. Mark Twain's homely maxim captures this: 'To a man with a hammer, everything looks like a nail'. One of the strangest things Rudolf Steiner said was that the thoughts of people today will determine the physical being of the world in the future, just as the thoughts of people in the past determined our earth today. Barfield echoes this with a little more phenomenological finesse. 'The future of the phenomenal world,' he warns, 'can no longer be regarded as entirely independent of man's volition'.[24] If we are what we eat, the world is what we think.

I say this not to induce in my readers a state of panic and anxiety, a paranoid concern about the thoughts in their heads, a worry that they shouldn't be thinking the thoughts they are thinking. Such neurotic fear is the opposite of the effect I would like these reflections to have. The world we are living in at present is in a state of flux, with old boundaries breaking down without new contours being established. There is a sense that anything can happen. Such times are, I believe, especially sensitive to the forces in play and a slight shift in some element may have an effect much wider and influential than one would have ever expected. There is, we can say, a kind of 'butterfly effect' in history, just as there is in the weather, with slight changes at one end resulting in larger ones at the other.[25]

It is at such times that something like Barfield's responsibility of the imagination is especially needed. This requires a calm, detached, but engaged awareness, the kind of 'passive potency' Swedenborg spoke of, an alert, self-possessed attention to detail and readiness to receive, with both ways of knowing available for work. It is in such a state of wakefulness and purpose that what we may have learned of the lost knowledge of the imagination can be of use to ourselves and to the world. To paraphrase Blake, in the future, the world's face as it unfolds it, will depend on the minds that behold it.

Notes

1. A Different Kind of Knowing

1   Karl Jaspers, *Way to Wisdom,* Ralph Manheim, trans. (London: Victor Gollancz, 1951) p. 98.
2   George Steiner, *Has Truth a Future?* (London: BBC Publications, 1978) pp. 16f.
3   John Shand, *Philosophy and Philosophers* (London: Penguin Books, 1994) p. 6.
4   He is generally referred to as Dionysius the Areopagite or as Pseudo-Dionysius. This is because he was confused with the Athenian converted by the apostle Paul and mentioned in Acts 17:34; he was also confused with St Dionysius (St Denis), the patron saint of France.
5   I tell the story of this unusual union in *The Quest for Hermes Trismegistus* (Edinburgh: Floris Books, 2011).
6   Jaspers 1951, p. 98.
7   Friedrich Nietzsche, *The Will to Power,* Walter Kaufman and R.J. Hollingdale trans. (New York: Random House, 1967) p. 8.
8   Steven Weinberg, *The First Three Minutes* (New York: Basic Books, 1993) p. 154.
9   Jacques Barzun, *From Dawn to Decadence* (New York: HarperCollins, 2000) p. 218.
10 Quoted in Colin Wilson, *Religion and the Rebel* (Cambridge, MA: Houghton Mifflin Co., 1957) p. 185.
11 Blaise Pascal, *Pensées* (New York: E.P. Dutton & Co, 1958) p. 1.
12 Barzun 2000, p. 216.
13 Ibid. p. 217.
14 Quoted in William Anderson, *Dante the Maker* (London: Routledge, 1980) p. 410.
15 Ernst Jünger, *The Adventurous Heart,* Thomas Friese trans. (Candor, NY: Telos Press Publishing, 2012) p. 12.
16 Michael Polanyi, *The Tacit Dimension* (New York: Anchor Books, 1967) p. 4.
17 One might say that we do 'half ride' it at first. We try to and fall down. But that is riding it badly. We don't 'half play' a musical instrument, but we can certainly play it badly.
18 Alfred North Whitehead, *Symbolism Its Meaning and Effect* (New York: G.P. Putnam's Sons, 1959). Whitehead actually speaks of 'causal efficacy' and 'presentational immediacy'; I am following the understandable rephrasing of Whitehead's terms which Wilson gives in *Beyond the Outsider* (Boston: Houghton Mifflin Co., 1965) For an extended discussion of Whitehead's ideas in the context of Wilson's philosophy see my book *Beyond the Robot: The Life and Work of Colin Wilson* (New York: Tarcher/Perigree, 2016).

19   Gary Lachman, *The Caretakers of the Cosmos* (Edinburgh: Floris Books, 2013) pp. 85 88.

20   See http://www.nature.com/news/the-split-brain-a-tale-of-two-halves-1.10213

21   I should point out that in recent times Peter Kingsley has done interesting work on the mythic roots of Greek philosophy. See for example Peter Kingsley, *In The Dark Places of Wisdom* (Inverness, CA; The Golden Sufi Center, 1999).

22   Francis Cornford, *From Religion to Philosophy* (Princeton, NJ: Princeton University Press, 1991) p. xiv.

23   Ibid.

24   George Steiner 1978, p. 16.

25   You may, in a variation of Dr Johnson's celebrated refutation of Bishop Berkeley, pick up a stone and say 'Here is matter.' If you do, I will answer, 'No, it is a stone.' Show me matter that is not stone, or tree, or cloud, or lake – matter, that is, that is not some 'thing' but simply itself. That, I say, you cannot do.

26   Barzun 2000, p. 218.

27   In the earliest versions of the myth, Orpheus succeeds in freeing Eurydice from Hades; it was only in later versions that he fails, and the tale becomes a tragedy.

28   Barzun 2000, p. 217.

29   See Lachman, *The Secret Teachers of the Western World*, (New York: Tarcher Penguin, 2015).

30   Jünger 2012, p. 12. Jacques Barzun *The House of Intellect* (New York: HarperCollins, 2002), originally published 1959.

31   See Lachman, 2015.

32   Kathleen Raine, *The Inner Journey of the Poet* (New York: George Braziller, 1982) p. 12.

33   Alfred North Whitehead, *Modes of Thought* (New York: The Free Press, 1966) p. 1.

34   William Blake, *The Marriage of Heaven and Hell* in *The Complete Poetry and Prose of William Blake,* ed. David V. Erdman, (Berkeley, CA; University of California Press, 1982) p. 38.

35   It is a phenomenon, in Sir William Grove's words, 'so obvious to simple apprehension that to define it would make it more obscure'. Quoted in Samuel Butler, 'Thought and Language' in *The Importance of Language,* ed. Max Black (Ithaca, NY: Cornell University Press, 1969) p. 13.

2. A Look Inside the World

1   This is a point that Maurice Nicoll made very well in his book *Living Time* (London: Watkins, 1981) in which he argues that we are, in essence, invisible.

2   This is the conclusion of Tor Norretrander's *The User Illusion* (New York: Penguin, 1999), one of many books whose aim, as its subtitle tells us, is to 'cut consciousness down to size'.

3   If we think about this we can see that it can lead to somewhat disturbing con- clusions. One is that my 'I', my sense of self, a very important part of my inside,

must not really exist. Nor must those of the scientists and philosophers writing books declaring that my inside or theirs doesn't really exist. What is really writing those books are the physical processes that create the illusion that there are individual 'I's' doing it. But for there to be an illusion, there must be someone being 'fooled' by it. The usual suspect here would be me. But if 'I' *am* the illusion, one wants to ask who it is that I am fooling? Another possibility is that, if there is no inside, then everything, all of reality, must only be an outside. But here are some logical problems here too. To have an 'outside' one must have an 'inside', just as in order to have a back one must have a front. Yet if there is no 'inside', and so no 'outside' what are we left with?

4   One criticism of this idea is the fact that unborn babies dream while still in the womb. If there is nothing in the mind that was not first in the senses, one wants to ask what these unborn children are dreaming about, given that their senses are not yet working, at least not in the way that they will be once they have left the womb. And even if we want to say that 'No, their senses are working and they are internalising sensations they receive through the mother', one wants to ask how *different* an experience their 'waking' and 'sleeping' can be? Engulfed in the warmth, darkness and comfort of the womb, there would not be a great deal for them to 'internalise', very little, that is, for them to 'photograph'. This suggests that these unborn dreamers may be dreaming about something like Jung's archetypes, inherent patterns of experience, they come 'furnished' with through their biological inheritance.

5   It is also linked to the production of the neurotransmitter serotonin.

6   Swedenborg, like Pascal, was another good geometer and intuiter.

7   See Gary Lachman, *Swedenborg: An Introduction to His Life and Ideas* (New York: Tarcher/Penguin, 2009).

8   Colin Wilson, *Beyond the Outsider* (Boston: Houghton Mifflin Co., 1965) p. 51.

9   Gary Lachman, *A Secret History of Consciousness* (Great Barrington, MA: Lindisfarne Books, 2003) pp. xxi–xxxv.

10   This interview was originally published in *Lapis* 3, 1996; it can be found in Gary Lachman *Revolutionaries of the Soul* (Wheaton, Il: Quest Books, 2014) pp. 43–82.

11   The pairing comes from the Greek poet Archilochus: 'The fox knows many things, the hedgehog knows one big thing'.

12   Owen Barfield, *Romanticism Comes of Age* (Middleton, CT: Wesleyan University Press, 1989) p. 189.

13   Owen Barfield, *Owen Barfield and the Origin of Language* (Spring Valley, NY: St. George Publications, 1976) p. 10.

14   Barfield's friend was Cecil Harwood, another member of the Inklings, a writer himself, and the founder of the first Waldorf school in England, the 'New School' which subsequently became Michael Hall.

15   Barfield 1976, p. 3.

16   Erich Heller, *In The Age of Prose* (Cambridge, UK: Cambridge University Press, 1984) 'The age of prose: this meant that … prose had become the ruling mode of perception'. p. 3.

17   Ibid. p.7.

18   'Make me they lyre, even as the forest is/What if my leaves are falling like its own?'

19 This does raise some complications when we consider that something we find 'breathtaking' – say some beautiful natural scenery – can also being 'inspiring'. It can take our breath away, but also give some to us.

20 Barfield 1976, p.5. Barfield has in mind the great orientalist Max Müller in particular, but people like John Locke and the French writer Anatole France espoused similar ideas.

21 Owen Barfield, *Poetic Diction* (Middleton, CT: Wesleyan University Press, 19887) p. 73.

22 Barfield 1976, p. 8.

23 Which is not to say that everyone today speaks and writes faultless prose. Hardly. It seems even that has deteriorated to the telegraphic Newspeak of text messaging and 'snap chats'. Orwell's nightmare of a language spoken by the larynx and not the mind – that is, automatically and with reduced meaning – seems not too far off.

24 Heller 1984, p. 3.

25 Heller and Barfield were not the only ones to consider this. The eighteenth-century Italian philosopher Giambattista Vico believed that human beings 'danced before they walked'. He also believed that 'poetry came before prose, and that men naturally embodied their feelings, attitudes, and thoughts in symbols'. According to the psychologist Anthony Storr, whom I am quoting, 'the metaphorical use of language, according to Vico, preceded the literal or scientific', and Storr mentions that a more recent philosopher, Martin Heidegger, felt the same. 'Poetry proper,' Heidegger says, 'is never merely a higher mode of everyday language. It is the reverse: everyday language is a forgotten and therefore used-up poem, from which there hardly resounds a call any longer'. In his essay on Vico, another philosopher, Isaiah Berlin – one not usually associated with Heidegger (and certainly not Barfield) – speaks similarly. 'A world in which men naturally talk of the lips of a vase, the teeth of a plough, the mouth of a river, a neck of land, handfuls of one thing, the heart of another, veins of minerals, bowels of the earth, murmuring waves, whistling winds and smiling skies, groaning tables and weeping willows {examples all take from Vico's *Scienza Nuova*} – such a world must be deeply and systematically different from any in which such phrases are felt, even remotely, to be metaphorical, as contrasted with so-called literal speech'. Anthony Storr, *Music and the Mind* (London: HarperCollins, 1997) pp. 12–13. Storr is quoting from Heidegger's essay 'Language', which is collected in *Poetry, Language, and Thought* (New York: HarperCollins, 2000) and Isaiah Berlin's *Vico and Herder* (London: Hogarth Press, 1976) pp. 46f. He also remarks that Jean Jacques Rousseau believed that the earliest languages were melodic and poetic rather than prosaic and practical.

26 Jean Gebser, *The Ever-Present Origin,* trans. Noel Barstad and Algis Mickunas (Athens, Ohio: Ohio University Press, 1985) pp. 12–15.

27 Barfield 1976, p. 9.

28 This is one of the arguments of *The Secret Teachers of the Western World* (New York: Tarcher Penguin, 2015). See especially pp. 18–21.

29 Ibid.

30 Barfield 1976, p. 9.

31 Martin Heidegger, 'Language' in *Poetry, Language, and Thought* (New York: HarperCollins, 2000).

32   Owen Barfield, *Speaker's Meaning* (Oxford, UK: Barfield Press, 2011) pp. 75–76.

33   Owen Barfield, *Saving the Appearances* (Middleton, CT: Wesleyan University Press, 1988) pp. 142, 182.

34   The idea that the world was created by God contracting Himself, limiting Himself, so as to allow a space for creation to take place, is part of the Lurianic tradition of Kabbalah. See Gary Lachman, *The Caretakers of the Cosmos* (Edinburgh, UK: Floris Books, 2013) pp. 31f.

35   Barfield 1988, pp. 122f.

36   Barfield 1976, p. 10.

37   As I point out in *A Secret History of Consciousness*, practically all creation myths are also myths about the creation of man, of, that is, self-consciousness. Lachman 2003, pp. 103–110.

38   Barfield 1989, p. 123.

39   Barfield 2011, p. 27.

40   Ibid. p. 37.

41   Colin Wilson, *Poetry and Mysticism* (San Francisco, CA: City Lights Books, 1970) pp. 53–55.

42   Barfield 2011, p. 29.

43   Jünger 2012, p. 16.

44   Ibid.

45   Ibid. p. 17.

46   Ibid. p. 3.

47   Ibid.

48   He would perhaps today ask, as the physicist David Bohm and others have, if it was like a holograph.

49   See Lachman 2015.

50   R. A. Schwaller de Lubicz, *Nature Word* (West Stockbridge, Mass; Lindisfarne Books, 1985) p. 135.

3. The Knower and the Known

1   John Armstrong, *Love, Life, Goethe* (London: Allen Lane, 2006) p. 295.

2   Johann Wolfgang von Goethe, *Italian Journey,* trans. W. H. Auden and Elizabeth Mayer (New York: Schocken Books, 1968) p. 5.

3   Johann Wolfgang von Goethe, *The Sorrows of Young Werther,* trans. Michael Hulse (London: Penguin Books, 1989) p. 65.

4   W.H. Auden and Elizabeth Mayer, *Introduction to Goethe* 1968, p. xvii.

5   J.F. Hendry, *The Sacred Threshold: A Life of Rilke* (Manchester, UK: Carcanet Press, 1983) p. 55.

6   Colin Wilson, *The Outsider as Musician* (Nottingham, UK: Paupers' Press, 1987) p. 1.

7   Johann Wolfgang von Goethe, *Autobiography* (Chicago: University of Chicago Press, 1974) pp. 40f.

8   Ronald Gray, *Goethe the Alchemist* (Cambridge: Cambridge University Press, 1952).

9   Abraham von Franckenberg, *The Life and Death of Jacob Boehme* at http://www.jacobboehmeonline.com/frankenberg

10   Quoted in Colin Wilson, *Religion and the Rebel* (Boston: Houghton and Mifflin, 1957) p. 154.

11   Goethe 1974, p. 371.

12   It held this status from 1647 to 1874, when it was surpassed by St Nikolai's Church, in Hamburg.

13   Goethe 1974, p. 416.

14   Ibid. p. 419.

15   Hans Gebert, 'About Goetheanistic Science' *Journal for Anthroposophy* (Spring 1979) pp. 45f, quoted in Robert McDermott, *The Essential Steiner* (San Francisco: Harper and Row, 1984) pp. 39f.

16   McDermott 1984, p. 40.

17   Goethe 1974, pp. 305f.

18   Ibid. p. 251.

19   Ibid. p. 383.

20   Arthur Koestler, *The Ghost in the Machine* (New York: The Macmillan Co., 1967) p. 138.

21   William Wordsworth, 'The Tables Turned' 1789 at https://www.poetryfoundation.org/poems-and-poets/poems/detail/45557

22   Quoted in Erich Heller, *The Disquiet Mind* (New York: Farrar, Straus, & Cudahy: 1957) p. 6. Italics in original. What Goethe was speaking of here was what Spinoza had called *natura naturans*, or 'nature 'naturing', nature in the active sense, rather than *natura naturata*, nature 'natured', nature as a finished product. The new mechanical science ignored *natura naturans* and focused solely on *natura naturata*.

23   Ibid. p. 7.

24   Ibid.

25   Johann Wolfgang von Goethe, *Maxims and Reflections* (London: Penguin Books, 1998) p. 155.

26   Ronald Brady, 'Goethe's Natural Science: Some Non-Cartesian Meditations', quoted in McDermott 1984, p. 38.

27   The irony in Huxley's remark is striking in that it is precisely the 'childlike' way of engaging with nature that the scientific method seeks to 'improve' by ridding it of its 'subjectivity'. The child engages with nature imaginatively, in the way that poets and mystics do among adults. For children, the border between their inner world and the outer one is porous; hence, with Blake, they can see heaven in a sunflower. Science tells them this is only their 'imagination' and that the sunflower is really a weed.

28   On this see my essay, 'The Spiritual Detective: How Baudelaire Invented Symbolism, by way of Swedenborg, E.T.A. Hoffmann and Edgar Allan Poe' in which I use Poe's 'The Purloined Letter' as a metaphor for a form of 'active seeing'. *Philosophy, Literature, Mysticism: An Anthology of Essays on Swedenborg* (London: The Swedenborg Society, 2013) pp. 217–32.

29   For a precise and detailed account of Goethe's method of observation one can do no better than to read Henri Bortoft, *The Wholness of Nature: Goethe's Way of Science* (Edinburgh, UK: Floris Books, 1996). A further and equally important study is Bortoft's *Taking Appearance Seriously* (Edinburgh, UK: Floris Books, 2014).

30   Quoted in Heller 1957, p. 14.

31   See Gary Lachman, *The Caretakers of the Cosmos* (Edinburgh, UK: Floris Books, 2013) pp. 111–15.

32   This 'dynamic' way of seeing has a history in European thought. See Bortoft
      *Taking Appearance Seriously: The Dynamic Way of Seeing in Goethe and European
      Thought* (Edinburgh, UK: Floris Books, 2014).
33   Jean-Paul Sartre, *The Transcendence of the Ego* (1936).
34   Paul Ricoeur in *Husserl: An Analysis of his Phenomenology* (Evanston,
      Il; Northwestern Univeristy Press, 2004) quoted in Colin Wilson,
      Superconsciousness (London: Watkins Books, 2009) p. 172. The British exis-
      tential philosopher Colin Wilson was another who understood the 'creative'
      character of Husserl's intentionality and he made it the centre of the 'new
      existentialism' he developed in the books of his 'Outsider cycle'. See my
      book, *Beyond the Robot: The Life and Work of Colin Wilson* (New York: Tarcher
      Perigee, 2016) for a detailed analysis of Wilson's ideas on consciousness
      and intentionality.
35   Husserl himself said that his aim in his phenomenological excavations was
      to uncover what he called the 'transcendental ego', the 'I' *behind* our everyday
      ego. By doing this he hoped to arrive at the 'keepers of the keys of being',
      who he related to 'the Mothers' who appear in Part Two of Goethe's drama
      of Western consciousness, *Faust*. The 'I' behind the everyday ego sounds
      rather like the Self of Eastern philosophy, a different centre of consciousness
      than the everyday left-brain ego. Heidegger, Husserl's student, shared with
      the esoteric teacher G. I. Gurdjieff the recognition that one method by which
      we may be shaken out of our 'forgetfulness of being' and made 'awake' is
      through a vivid realisation of the eventuality of our death. Though phenom-
      enology and spiritual teachings seem on the surface to have little in common,
      they do share a concern with 'authentic being' and experiencing our true 'I'.
36   Both Goethe and Blake were unaware of Newton's profound concern with
      alchemy and other aspects of Western esotericism. Although well-known
      to Newton's contemporaries, these aspects of his career only came to light
      in 1936 , when the economist John Maynard Keynes bought a collection of
      Newton's papers and quickly realised that the father of modern science –
      and the modern world – spent more time thinking and writing about
      alchemy than he did gravity. See Lachman 2015, pp. 302f.
37   No one except Rudolf Steiner who as a young man edited Goethe's scien-
      tific writings and later based his own philosophy of 'super-sensible percep-
      tion' on Goethe's ideas. See McDermott 1984, pp. 37–41. The philosopher
      Ludwig Wittgenstein also took Goethe's colour theory seriously. See
      Ludwig Wittgenstein, *Remarks on Colour* (Berkeley, CA: University
      of California Press, 1978).
38   Again, see Bortoft 2013, pp. 29–68.
39   Goethe speaking to Eckermann, quoted in Heller 1957, p. 31.
40   Quoted in McDermott 1984, p. 49.
41   Rudolf Steiner, *On the Theory of Knowledge Implicit in Goethe's World
      Conception* (1886), quoted in Colin Wilson, *Rudolf Steiner: The Man and his
      Vision* (Wellingborough, UK: The Aquarian Press, 1987) p. 166.
42   *Wär nicht das Auge sonnenhaft/Wie könnten wir das Licht erblicken?/Lebt' nicht in
      uns des Gottes eigne Kraft,/Wie könnt uns Göttliches entzücken?* From Book Three
      of *Tame Xenia* ,'Tame Reminders'.
43   Goethe 1998, p. 67.
44   Quoted in Friedrich Nietzsche, *Untimely Meditations,* trans. R. J. Hollingdale
      (Cambridge, UK: Cambridge University Press, 1983) p. 59.

45   Heller 1957, p.20.

46   Ibid. p.21.

47   Ibid.

48   Koestler 1967, p. 138.

49   Goethe's friend Schiller did this too. His *Letters on the Aesthetic Education of Man* (1794) form an early guide book in reconciling and transcending the opposition between the analytical and creative drives – or left and right brain – in human consciousness. For Novalis see Lachman 2015, pp. 350f.

50   Quoted in Walter Lowrie, *Religion of a Scientist: Selections for Gustav Fechner* (New York: Pantheor Books, 1946) p. 211. I write about Fechner in Lachman 2013, pp. 167–70.

51   Peter Watson, *The German Genius* (London: Simon and Schuster, 2010) p. 201.

52   Antoine Faivre, *Access to Western Esotericism* (Albany, NY: SUNY Press, 1994) p. 83; Novalis, *Pollen and Fragments,* Arthur Versluis, trans. (Grand Rapids, Mich. Phanes Press, 1989) p. 71.

53   Friedrich Wilhelm Joseph Von Schelling in *German Idealist Philosophy,* Rüdiger Bubner, ed. (London: Penguin Books, 1997) p. 209.

4. The Way Within

1   The 'twelve dead' eventually became the source of Jung's strange Gnostic work, *The Seven Sermons of the Dead*. See Gary Lachman, *Jung the Mystic* (NY: Tarcher/Penguin, 2010) pp. 122–24.

2   Jung was not the only one at this time to receive portents of the coming disaster. In 1912 the German Expressionist painter Ludwig Meidner pro-duced a series of 'Apocalyptic Landscapes' that depicted cities laid to waste. In them Meidner painted comets shooting across the sky, a black sun, men and women running screaming through the streets and buildings collaps-ing. Meidner painted this works in a brief burst of inspiration; his later work lacks the intensity of these disturbing canvases. One may speculate that the same prophetic genius that gripped Meidner also came to Jung. http://weimarart.blogspot.co.uk/2010/07/ludwig-meidner.html

3   Henri Ellenberger, *The Discovery of the Unconscious* (London: Fontana Press, 1994) p. 673.

4   Philemon was a Christian who received a letter from St Paul, the Epistle to Philemon, found in the New Testament.

5   For example, while working on his painting of Philemon, Jung came across a dead kingfisher along Lake Zürich. The birds are rare in Zürich and Jung had never come across one, let alone a dead one. Jung was also very inter-ested in the Grail legends, one character of which is the Fisher King.

6   C.G. Jung, *Memories, Dreams, Reflections* (London: Fontana Paperbacks, 1989) p. 207.

7   C.G. Jung, *Analytical Psychology: Notes of the Seminar Given in 1925* (London: Routledge, 1992) p. 38.

8   Aldous Huxley, *The Doors of Perception* and *Heaven and Hell* (London: Grafton Books, 1987) pp. 69f.

9   See Gary Lachman, *Swedenborg: An Introduction to His Life and Ideas*
      (New York: Tarcher/Penguin 2012) p. 91.

10   Quoted in Henri Corbin, *Creative Imagination in the Sufism of Ibn 'Arqbi*
      (Princeton, NJ: Princeton University Press, 1969) p. 179.

11   W.B. Yeats, *The Collected Letter of W. B. Yeats*, vol III (Oxford, UK: Oxford
      University Press, 1994) p. 40.

12   Barfield 1957, p. 137.

13   Ibid.

14   Christopher Bamford, 'Esotericism Today: The Example of Henry Corbin'
      in Henry Corbin, *The Voyage and the Messenger* (Berkeley, CA: North Atlantic
      Books, 1998) p. xxvi.

15   See Gary Lachman, *The Quest for Hermes Trismegistus* (Edinburgh, UK:
      Floris Books, 2011) pp. 109–121.

16   Quoted in Corbin, 1998 p. xxix.

17   Ethan Kleinberg, *Generation Existential: Heidegger's Philosophy in France 1927–
      1961* (Ithaca, NY: Cornell University Press, 2007) p. 70. Corbin was also
      close friends with Alexandre Kojeve, whose lectures on Hegel at the École
      Pratique des Hautes Études in the 1930s had a powerful impact on existen-
      tialism. See Alexandre Kojeve, *Introduction to the Reading of Hegel* (Ithaca,
      NY: Cornell University Press, 1980).

18   Martin Heidegger, 'On the Essence of Truth' in *Basic Writings* (New York:
      Harper & Row, 1977) p. 132.

19   Isiah Berlin, *The Magus of the North* (NY: Farrar, Straus, & Giroux, 1994).

20   Johann Georg Hamann, *Aesthetica in Nuce* (Cambridge University Press) p. 2.
      http://assets.cambridge.org/97805218/06398/excerpt/9780521806398_excerpt.pdf

21   As with *Naturphilosophie* English does not have a direct equivalent for the
      German *Sprachphilosophie* which differs from Anglo-American 'philosophy of
      language' in the same way that *Naturphilosophie* differs from 'natural philoso-
      phy'. See George Steiner, *Extraterritorial* (NY: Atheneum, 1976) pp. x–xi.

22   George Steiner, *After Babel* (London: Oxford University Press, 1975)
      pp. 76f.

23   Ernst Cassirer, *The Philosophy of Symbolic Forms, Vol. 1: Language* (New
      Haven, CT: Yale University Press, 1975) pp. 150f.

24   Corbin 1998, pp. xxxii–xxxiii.

25   Ibid. p. xlvii.

26   See especially *The Man of Light in Iranian Sufism*, *Cyclical Time and Ismaili
      Gnosis*, and *The Voyage and the Messenger*.

27   Henry Corbin, *Mundus imaginalis* or *The Imaginary and the Imaginal* (Ipswich,
      UK: Golgonooza Press, 1976) pp. 3, 10.

28   Ibid. p. 9.

29   http://phys.org/news/2013–09-scientists-never-before-seen.html

30   Corbin, 1976 p. 14.

31   Lachman 2010, pp. 115–21.

32   Corbin 1976, p. 6.

33   Some researchers quibble about this, arguing that waking from sleep,
      what they call the 'hypnopompic state' differs from falling into it. There
      are indeed differences, but in a general sense we can say that for our pur-
      poses the two are similar enough to consider them identical. The most

exhaustive study of the hypnagogic state is Andreas Mavromatis, *Hypnagogia* (London: Routledge, 1987). I have written about it at length in *A Secret History of Consciousness* (Great Barrington, MA: Lindisfarne Books, 2003) pp. 85–94. A short article of mine on the subject can be found here http://www.mindpowernews.com/Hypagogic.htm

34   Lachman 2010, pp. 27, 119f.
35   Lachman 2012, p. 87.
36   Emanuel Swedenborg, *Heaven and Hell* (New York; Swedenborg Foundation, 1984).
37   Herbert Silberer, 'Report on a Method of Eliciting and Observing Certain Symbolic Hallucination-Phenomena' in *Organisation and Pathology of Thought* ed. David Rapaport (New York: Columbia University Press, 1951).
38   Henry Corbin, *Swedenborg and Esoteric Islam* (New York; Swedenborg Foundation, 2006).
39   Swedenborg, 1984, p. 81.
40   Czeslaw Milosz, Introduction to *The Noble Traveller: The Life and Writings of O.V. de L. Milosz* (West Stockbridge, MA: Lindisfarne Books, 1985) p. 33.
41   Bamford in Corbin 1998, p. xvi.
42   See Lachman, 'The Spiritual Detective: How Baudelaire Invented Symbolism, by way of Swedenborg, E.T.A Hoffmann, and Edgar Allan Poe' in *Philosophy, Literature, Mysticism: An Anthology of Essays on Swedenborg* (London: The Swedenborg Society, 2013).
43   Gary Lachman, *Rudolf Steiner: An Introduction to His Life and Work* (New York: Tarcher/Penguin, 2007) p. 149.
44   Corbin 1976, p. 7.
45   Ibid. p. 13.
46   Ibid. p. 15.
47   Ibid. p. 20.
48   Goethe 1974, pp. 305f.
49   Henry Corbin, *Spiritual Body and Celestial Earth: From Mazdean Iran to Shi'ite Tran,* trans. Nancy Pearson (London: IB Tauris & Co. Ltd, 1990) pp. 10f.
50   Ibid.
51   Corbin 1976, p. 18.
52   Ibid.
53   Ibid.

5. *The Learning of the Imagination*

1   Erich Kahler *The Disintegration of Form in the Arts* (New York: George Braziller, 1968) p. 3.
2   Ibid. p. 23.
3   Although with crystals we see the introduction of form into the inorganic, which gives rise to the speculation, common to *Naturphilosopie*, that at this level the organic and inorganic share some middle ground.
4   Kahler 1968, p. 4.
5   Ibid. p. 5.
6   Ibid. p. 20.
7   Ibid. pp. 27f.

8   Ibid. p. 95.

9   Jacques Barzun, 'Liberalism and the Religion of Art' in *Critical Questions* (Chicago, IL: University of Chicago Press, 1982) p. 173.

10   With Jean-Paul Sartre, Simone de Beauvoir was one of the leading lights of French existentialism. In his essay 'Anti-Sartre', collected in *Below the Iceberg* (San Bernadino, CA: Borgo Press, 1998), Colin Wilson tells the story of some students who approached Sartre after he had given a resounding lecture on freedom. This was soon after the liberation of Paris and the defeat of the Nazis. The students were enthused with Sartre's celebration of freedom, and inspired by his words, they asked the philosopher what they should do with their freedom. Sartre replied, in effect, 'You can do what you like'. The students walked away somewhat less inspired. Freedom is not enough. It must be joined to some purpose or aim to be of value. Sartre's 'do what you like' encapsulates the moral vacuum in which his version of existentialism – the most popular – existed and is the equivalent of running out of barriers to break down with the resultant sense of pointlessness.

11   Ibid. pp. 174f.

12   Jacques Barzun, *The Use and Abuse of Art* (Princeton, NJ: Princeton University Press, 1973).

13   William Barrett, *Time of Need: Forms of Imagination and Their Time* (New York: Harper and Row, 1972) p. 10.

14   Ibid. p. 23.

15   Art vandalism, a step up from irony and sarcasm, is a more intense form of defacing great works as an expression of protest. http://www.telegraph.co.uk/culture/art/art-features/9593748/When-art-gets-vandalised.html

16   Erich Heller, *The Artist's Journey into the Interior* (New York: Harcourt, Brace, Jovanovich, 1976) pp. 134f.

17   Ibid. p. 135.

18   Barrett recognised that this apparent scattering of artistic energies may not be as troubling a sign as Heller believed. 'From the oriental point of view,' he writes, 'the distinction between grand and insignificant, high and low, belongs only to the relative world of practical realities. From a deeper point of view, any object may mirror the world, and the deepest revelations may come through the apparently most trivial things or people'. (Barrett 1972, p. 199). Proust's madeleine can be understood in a context other than that of a brief affair with the 'Don Juan of the creative spirit'. Blake, we know, saw a world in a grain of sand and heaven in a wild flower. For an understanding of what the 'transfiguration of the commonplace' may mean in the context of a philosophy of consciousness based on Husserl's phenomenology, see Colin Wilson, *Poetry and Mysticism* (San Francisco, CA: City Lights Books, 1969). For an overview of Wilson's ideas about consciousness, see Gary Lachman, *Beyond the Robot: The Life and Work of Colin Wilson* (New York: Tarcher Perigee, 2016). Rilke's house, bridge, fountain and gate are offered to his Angel in the Ninth of his *Duino Elegies*.

19   Kathleen Raine, *Autobiographies* (London; Skoob Books Publishing, 1991) p. 2.

20   Ibid. p. 4.

21   Ibid.

22   Ibid.

23   Ibid. p. 117.
24   Ludwig Wittgenstein, *Tractatus Logico-Philosophicus,* trans. D.F. Pears and B. F. McGuiness (London: Routledge & Kegan Paul, 1969) p. 151. For Wittgenstein and Broch see Allan Janik and Stephen Toulmain, *Wittgenstein's Vienna* (New York: Simon & Schuster, 1973). For an account of the effect of logical positivism, and its offspring, linguistic analysis, on modern philosophy see Bryan Magee, *Confessions of a Philosopher* (London: Phoenix Books, 1997).
25   Raine 1991, p. 135.
26   Ibid. p. 131.
27   Kathleen Raine, *Blake and Tradition* (London: Routledge, 1969).
28   Kathleen Raine, *Defending Ancient Springs* (West Stockbridge. MA: Lindisfarne Books, 1985.) p. 157.
29   Ibid.
30   Ibid. p. 166.
31   Ibid. p. 165.
32   Ibid. p. 158.
33   Ibid.
34   Ibid. p. 159.
35   Ibid. p. 169.
36   Ibid. p. 159.
37   Ibid. p. 160.
38   I should point out that the Tradition Raine speaks of, while sharing much with the Traditionalism of René Guénon and his followers, is still of a very different sort. Put briefly, where Guénon and other Traditionalists refer to Tradition as a kind of authority, 'the Law' as it were, that has become lost in the modern world, although remnants of it may still be found in the major religions, Raine sees Tradition in the sense of a body of knowledge and symbols relating to what we can call the 'reality of the imagination'. In an interview I did with Raine in 1997 she said as much, remarking that she felt that Guénon had no imagination.
39   I should mention that, as William Barrett did, Raine realised that beauty could be found outside Tradition. It was 'an aspect that absolutely anything in the world may assume when seen in a certain way'. Kathleen Raine, *The Underlying Order and Other Essays* (London: The Temenos Academy, 2008) p. 58.
40   Raine 1967, p. 169.
41   Ibid. p. 160.
42   Kathleen Raine, *Blake and Tradition* (London: Routledge, 2002) pp. xxviii–xxix.
43   Kathleen Raine in Raine and George Mills Harper ed., *Thomas Taylor The Platonist: Selected Writings* (Princeton, N. J.: Princeton University Press, 1969) p. 6.
44   The long and detailed history of the magical use of imagination, reaching back to the late Neoplatonists, through the Renaissance mages and 'magical memory', to the 'assumption of the god forms' that made up a great deal of the Golden Dawn teaching is, sadly, except for this mention, beyond the scope of this book.
45   Kathleen Raine, *W.B. Yeats and the Learning of the Imagination* (Ipswich, UK: Golgonooza Press, 1999) pp. 40, 55.
46   https://www.poetryfoundation.org/poems-and-poets/poems/detail/43291

47 https://www.poetryfoundation.org/poems-and-poets/poems/detail/43290

48 Colin Wilson, *The Occult* (New York: Random House, 1971) p. 108.

49 Kathleen Raine, *The Inner Journey of the Poet* (New York: George Braziller, 1982) p. 161. It may be the case that Keats' identification with the sparrow, and other poetic, sensitive people's similar *participation* with what they observe, may be linked to what are known as 'mirror neurons' which are located in Broca's area, the motor speech area of the brain's frontal lobe which are involved in watching someone perform an action and in imitating it. See McGilchrist 2010, p. 58.

50 Corbin 1976, p. 14.

51 Raine 1999, p. 92.

52 S. Foster Damon, *A Blake Dictionary* (Boulder, CO: Shambhala Publications, 1979) p. 396.

53 At least one later critic thought well of Taylor's work, suggesting that his rendition of the *Timaeus* was 'in certain respects closer than Jowett's to the flavour of the Greek'. Benjamin Jowett was a nineteenth-century scholar whose translations of Plato set the standard for many years. George Steiner *After Babel* (London: Oxford University Press, 1975) p. 345, n. 2.

54 Raine 1982, p. 15.

55 Marsilio Ficino was a young Greek scholar who, in 1462, was commissioned by the Florentine power broker Cosmio de' Medici to start his own Platonic Academy in a villa in the hills above Florence. Ficino translated much of Plato, lost during the Dark Ages, and also the *Corpus Hermeticum*, thus initiating what the historian Frances Yates called the 'Hermetic Renaissance'. Ficino taught a version of the 'perennial philosophy' which informed much of western occult, magical, and esoteric tradition that followed. See Gary Lachman, *The Quest for Hermes Trismegistus* (Edinburgh, UK: Floris Books, 2011).

56 Thomas Taylor, *Eleusinian and Bacchic Mysteries*, 'Introduction' quoted in Kathleen Raine, *Golgonooza, City of Imagination* (Husdon, NY: Lindisfarne Books, 1991) p. 3.

57 John Livingstone Lowes, *The Road to Xanadu* (London: Pan Books, 1978) p. 211.

58 Ibid.

59 Raine 1985, p. 95.

60 Raine 1982, p. 52.

61 Raine 1985, p. 97.

62 http://www.online-literature.com/coleridge/biographia-literaria/13/

63 Ibid.

64 Owen Barfield, *What Coleridge Thought* (Middleton, CT. Wesleyan University Press, 1971) p. 36.

65 Ibid. p. 35.

66 Richard Holmes, *Coleridge: Darker Reflections* (London: Flamingo Books, 1999) p. 129.

67 Barfield 1971, p. 89.

68 Ibid. p. 66.

69 https://www.poetryfoundation.org/resources/learning/essays/detail/69385

70 Barfield 1971, p. 87.

71 Colin Wilson used the same term to refer to a similar, if not identical power. See Lachman 2013, pp. 196–200 and Lachman 2016, pp. 253f.

72   Barfield 1971, p. 112.
73   Coleridge's distinction between 'understanding' and 'reason' came from his reading in German metaphysics, in which understanding is known as *Verstand* and reason *Vernunft*.
74   Barfield 1971, p. 121.
75   Such self-contemplation should be seen in the context of Henry Corbin's similar insights, mentioned in Chapter Four: 'The soul,' Corbin writes, is 'capable of perceiving concrete things whose existence ... constitutes *eo ipso* the very concrete existential form of these things'. That is to say that with these phenomena 'consciousness and its object are ontologically inseparable'.

6. The Responsible Imagination

1   See, for example, Andrei Tarkovsky's beautifully disturbing existential science-fiction film *Solaris* (1972).
https://www.theguardian.com/film/2010/oct/21/solaris-tarkovsky-science-fiction
2   http://quoteinvestigator.com/2013/01/01/einstein-imagination/
3   Ibid. Strangely enough, George Sylvester Viereck was at one time an associate of the notorious dark magician Aleister Crowley, during Crowley's years in New York during the First World War. See Gary Lachman, *Aleister Crowley: Magick, Rock and Roll, and the Wickedest Man in the World* (New York: Tarcher/Penguin, 2014) pp. 195–98.
4   Bernard Shaw, *The Complete Plays of Bernard Shaw* (London: Odhams Press, Ltd, 1934) p. 858.
5   http://quoteinvestigator.com/2013/01/01/einstein-imagination/ (My italics).
6   https://en.wikipedia.org/wiki/21st_Century_Schizoid_Man McGilchrist 2009 pp. 52f, 212f.
7   Lachman 2015, pp. 18–21.
8   Lachman 2011, pp. 180–82.
9   See Gary Lachman, *Turn Off Your Mind: The Dedalus Book of the 1960s* (Sawtry, UK: Dedalus Books, 2009).
10   Damien Hirst's *The Physical Impossibility of Death in the Mind of Someone Living* features a shark preserved in formaldehyde in a display case. Tracey Emin's *My Bed* features a bed she remained in for several days in a depressed state during which she ate nothing and drank only alcohol. Both works sold for huge sums at auction. Banksy, the pseudonym of an unidentified 'graffiti artist' spray paints buildings. He has in this way amassed an estimated fortune of $20 million.
11   https://www.psychologytoday.com/articles/200109/why-america-loves-reality-tv
12   This aphorism is also attributed to Marshall McLuhan
https://mcluhangalaxy.wordpress.com/2011/12/08/andy-warhol-marshall-mcluhan-the-artist-the-visionary/
13   For a study of how changes in styles of art anticipate changes in our 'picture' of the world see Leonard Shlain, *Art and Physics: Parallel Visions in Space, Time & Light* (New York: Quill William Morrow, 1991).
14   Barfield 1988, p. 146.

15   With this in mind we should consider the phenomena of *tulpas* and *egregores*,
      two different but related examples of what we can call 'thought forms'.
      A *tulpa* is a kind of imagined entity or being that is brought into existence
      through prolonged, persistent, and intense meditation and visualisation.
      In *Magic and Mystery in Tibet* the traveller Alexander David-Neal tells a classic
      tale of what happens when one gets out of one's control. An *egregore* is a kind
      of group entity that is maintained by the belief, ritual, sacrifice, and imagina-
      tion of its devotees. With enough of these, the *egregore* can take on a life of its
      own. See Joscelyn Godwin, *The Golden Thread* (Wheaton, IL: Quest Books,
      2007) pp. 47–54.
16   John Cowper Powys, *Autobiography* (London: Picador, 1982) p. 408.
17   Aleister Crowley, *Magick in Theory and Practice* (New York: Dover Books,
      1976) p. xii.
18   They were of course not alone nor the first. Rousseau and Goethe are here
      too. I am speaking, as Barfield did, of the change appearing in English litera-
      ture. Even here Wordsworth and Coleridge were anticipated somewhat by
      Mary Wollstonecraft. Her *Letters Written During a Short Residence in Sweden,
      Norway, and Denmark* (1796) display the kind of contemplative delight in
      nature and sensitivity to the 'sublime' – its strangeness and mystery – that
      Romanticism would make widely popular.
19   Petrarch, 'The Ascent of Mount Ventoux' in *Selections From the Canzoniere*
      (Oxford, UK: Oxford University Press, 1985) pp. 11–19.
20   Barfield 1988, pp. 145f.
21   Lachman 2010, pp. 241f, 246.
22   Lachman 2016, p. 171.
23   A.R. Orage *Consciousness: Animal, Human, Superman* (New York; Samuel
      Weiser, 1974) p. 68.
24   Barfield 1988, p. 160.
25   The 'butterfly effect' comes out of chaos theory and argues that slight varia-
      tions in what it calls 'initial conditions' can eventually have huge effects. So
      a butterfly flapping its wings in one part of the globe can cause a tornado
      in another.

Further Reading

Anderson, William (1980) *Dante the Maker*, London: Routledge.

Armstrong, John (2006) *Love, Life, Goethe*, London: Allen Lane.

Barfield, Owen (1971) *What Coleridge Thought*, Middleton, CT: Wesleyan University Press.

—, (1976) *Owen Barfield and the Origin of Language*, Spring Valley, NY: St George Publications.

—, (1988) *Poetic Diction*, Middleton, CT: Wesleyan University Press.

—, (1988) *Saving the Appearances*, Middleton, CT: Wesleyan University Press.

—, (1989) *Romanticism Comes of Age*, Middleton, CT: Wesleyan University Press.

—, (2011) *Speaker's Meaning*, Oxford, UK: Barfield Press.

Barrett, William (1972) *Time of Need: Forms of Imagination and Their Time*, New York: Harper & Row.

Barzun, Jacques (1973) *The Use and Abuse of Art*, Princeton, NJ: Princeton University Press.

—, (1982) *Critical Questions*, Chicago, IL: University of Chicago Press.

—, (2000) *From Dawn to Decadence*, New York: HarperCollins.

Bortoft, Henri (1996) *The Wholeness of Nature: Goethe's Way of Science*, Edinburgh, UK: Floris Books.

—, (2014) *Taking Appearance Seriously*, Edinburgh, UK: Floris Books.

Cassirer, Ernst (1975) *The Philosophy of Symbolic Forms*, New Haven, CT: Yale University Press.

Corbin, Henry (1969) *Creative Imagination in the Sufism of Ibn 'Arabi*, Princenton, NJ: Princeton University Press.

—, (1976) *Mundus Imaginalis or The Imaginary and the Imaginal*, Ipswich, UK: Golgonooza Press.

—, (1990) *Spiritual Body and Celestial Earth*, London: I.B. Tauris & Co.

—, (1998) *The Voyage and the Messenger*, Berkeley, CA: North Atlantic Books.

—, (2006) *Swedenborg and Esoteric Islam*, New York; Swedenborg Foundation.

Cornford, Francis (1991) *From Religion to Philosophy*, Princeton, NJ: Princeton University Press.

Ellenberger, Henri (1994) *The Discovery of the Unconscious*, London: Fontana.

Faivre, Antoine (1994) *Access to Western Esotericism*, Albany, NY: State University of New York Press.

Gebser, Jean (1985) *The Ever-Present Origin*, Athens, Ohio: Ohio University Press.

Goethe, Johann Wolfgang von (1968) *Italian Journey*, New York; Schocken Books.

—, (1974) *Autobiography*, Chicago, IL: University of Chicago Press.

—, (1988) *Maxims and Reflections*, London: Penguin Books.

—, (1989) *The Sorrows of Young Werther*, London: Penguin Books.

Gray, Roland (1952) *Goethe the Alchemist*, Cambridge, UK: Cambridge University Press.

Heidegger, Martin (1977) *Basic Writings*, New York: Harper & Row.

—, (2000) *Poetry, Language and Thought*, New York: HarperCollins.

Heller, Erich (1957) *The Disinherited Mind*, New York: Farrar, Strauss & Cudahy.

—, (1976) *The Artist's Journey Into the Interior*, New York: Harcourt, Brace, Jovanovich.

—, (1984) *In The Age of Prose*, Cambridge, UK: Cambridge University Press.

Hendry, J. F. (1983) *The Sacred Threshold: A Life of Rilke*, Manchester, UK: Carcanet Press.

Huxley, Aldous (1987) *The Doors of Perception and Heaven and Hell*, London: Grafton Books.

Jaspers, Karl (1951) *Way to Wisdom*, London: Gollancz.

Jung, Carl Gustav (1989) *Memories, Dreams, Reflections*, London: Fontana.

—, (1992) *Analytical Psychology: Notes on the Seminar Given in 1925*, London: Routledge.

Jünger, Ernst (2012) *The Adventurous Heart*, Candor, NY: Telos Press Publishing.

Kahler, Erich (1968) *The Disintegration of Form in the Arts*, New York: George Braziller.

Kingsley, Peter (1999) *In the Dark Places of Wisdom*, Inverness, CA: Golden Sufi Center.

Koestler, Arthur (1967) *The Ghost in the Machine*, New York: Macmillan & Co.

Lachman, Gary (2003) *A Secret History of Consciousness*, Great Barrington, MA: Lindisfarne Books.

—, (2007) *Rudolf Steiner: An Introduction to His Life and Work*, New York: Tarcher/Penguin.

—, (2009) *Turn Off Your Mind: The Dedalus Book of the 1960s*, Sawtry, UK: Dedalus Books.

—, (2010) *Jung the Mystic*, New York: Tarcher/Penguin.

—, (2011) *The Quest for Hermes Trismegistus*, Edinburgh, UK: Floris Books.

—, (2012) *Swedenborg: An Introduction to his Life and Ideas*, New York: Tarcher/Penguin and Edinburgh, UK: Floris Books.

—, (2013) *The Caretakers of the Cosmos*, Edinburgh, UK: Floris Books.

—, (2014) *Revolutionaries of the Soul*, Wheaton, IL: Quest Books.

—, (2015) *The Secret Teachers of the Western World*, New York: Tarcher/Penguin.

—, (2016) *Beyond the Robot: The Life and Work of Colin Wilson*, New York: Tarcher/Perigee.

Lowes, John Livingstone (1978) *The Road to Xanadu*, London: Pan Books.

Lowrie, Walter (1946) *Religion of a Scientist: Selections for Gustav Fechner*, New York: Pantheon Books.

McDermott, Robert (2010) *The New Essential Steiner*, Great Barrington, MA: Lindisfarne Books.

McGilchrist, Iain (2010) *The Master and His Emissary*, London: Yale University Press.

Nicoll, Maurice (1981) *Living Time*, London: Watkins Books.
Nietzsche, Friedrich (1967) *The Will to Power*, New York: Random House.
Pascal, Blaise (1958) *Pensées*, New York: E.P. Dutton & Co.
Polanyi, Michael (1967) *The Tacit Dimension*, New York: Anchor Books.
Raine, Kathleen (1969) *Blake and Tradition*, London: Routledge.
—, (1982) *The Inner Journey of the Poet*, New York: George Braziller.
—, (1985) *Defending Ancient Springs*, West Stockbridge, MA: Lindisfarne Books.
—, (1991) *Autobiographies*, London; Skoob Books Publishing.
—, (1991) *Golgonooza, City of Imagination*, Hudson, NY: Lindisfarne Books.
—, (1999) *W.B. Yeats and the Learning of the Imagination*, Ipswich, UK:
    Golgonooza Press.
—, (2008) *The Underlying Order and Other Essays*, London: Temenos
    Academy.
Schwaller de Lubicz, René (1984) *Nature Word*, West Stockbridge, MA:
    Lindisfarne Books.
Shand, John (1994) *Philosophy and Philosophers*, London: Penguin Books.
Steiner, George (1975) *After Babel*, Oxford, UK: Oxford University Press.
—, (1976) *Extraterritorial*, New York; Atheneum.
—, (1978) *Has Truth a Future?* London: BBC Publications.
Storr, Anthony (1999) *Music and the Mind*, London: HarperCollins.
Weinberg, Steven (1993) *The First Three Minutes*, New York: Basic Books.
Whitehead, Alfred North (1959) *Symbolism: Its Meaning and Effect*, New York:
    George Putnam's Sons.
—, (1966) *Modes of Thought*, New York: The Free Press.
Wilson, Colin (1957) *Religion and the Rebel*, Cambridge, MA: Houghton
    Mifflin.
—, (1965) *Beyond the Outsider*, Boston: Houghton Mifflin.
—, (1970) *The Occult*, New York: Random House.
—, (1970) *Poetry and Mysticism*, San Francisco, CA: City Lights Books.
—, (1987) *The Outsider as Musician*, Nottingham, UK: Pauper's Press.
—, (1987) *Rudolf Steiner: The Man and His Vision*, Wellingborough, UK:
    Aquarian Press.
—, (2009) *Superconsciousness*, London: Watkins Books.

Index

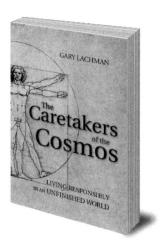

The Quest For Hermes Trismegistus
From Ancient Egypt to the Modern World

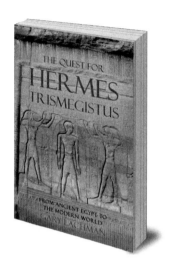

"An excellent addition to any history collection."
Midwest Book Review

"Lachman is an easy to read author yet has a near
encyclopaedic knowledge of esotericism."
Living Traditions Magazine

Considered by some a contemporary of Moses and a forerunner
of Christ, the almost mythical figure of Hermes Trismegistus
was thought to have walked with gods and be the source of
the divine wisdom granted to man at the dawn of time.

Gary Lachman brings to life the mysterious character of this
great spiritual guide, exposing the many theories and stories
surrounding him, and revitalizing his teachings for the
modern world.

Also available as an eBook

florisbooks.co.uk

Rudolf Steiner
An Introduction to His Life and Work

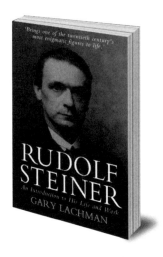

"[Gary Lachman] has rendered a great service
to Steiner and his movement."
Scientific and Medical Network Review

"Brings one of the twentieth century's
most enigmatic figures to life."
Booklist

Rudolf Steiner – educator, architect, artist, philosopher and
agriculturalist – ranks amongst the most creative and prolific
figures of the early twentieth century. Yet he remains a
mystery to most people.

Gary Lachman tells Steiner's story lucidly and with great
insight in the first truly popular biography, written by a
sympathetic but critical outsider. He presents Steiner's key
ideas in a readable, accessible way, tracing his beginning as
a young intellectual to the founding of his own metaphysical
teaching, called anthroposophy.

Also available as an eBook

florisbooks.co.uk

A Secret History of Consciousness

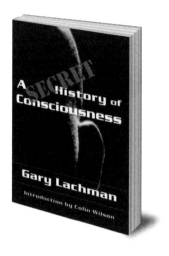

"Sophisticated and impressive."

Mike Jay, *Fortean Times*

"A marvellously exhilarating gallop through every
important modern theory of consciousness."

Colin Wilson, author of *The Occult and Mysteries*

What is consciousness like? How can consciousness be
achieved? Gary Lachman argues that consciousness is not
a result of neurons and molecules, but is actually responsible
for them. Meaning, he proposes, is not imported from the
outer world, but rather creates the world.

Concentrating on the late nineteenth-century onwards,
Lachman exposes the 'secret history' of consciousness
through thinkers such as P. D. Ouspensky Rudolf Steiner,
and Colin Wilson, as well as more mainstream philosophers
including Henri Bergson, William James, Owen Barfield
and psychologist Andreas Mavromatis.

Also available as an eBook

florisbooks.co.uk

Floris
Books

For news on all our **latest books**,
and to receive **exclusive discounts**,
join our mailing list at:

florisbooks.co.uk

Plus subscribers get a FREE book
with every online order!